Driver and rider training from RAC

# Get a free driving less...

## when you book 10 le...

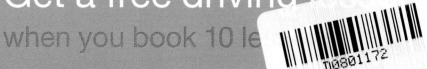

D0801172

## Plus get a free
## 'map' CD-ROM

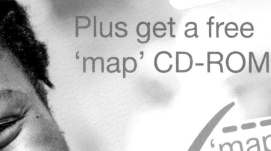

'map'
Guaranteed to improve
your chances of passing*

*Those who have used the 'map' CD-ROM had a 16% higher pass
rate in the Practical Test than those who didn't (BSM research, 2003).

# BSM

**the Best Start in Motoring**

# More value at no extra cost...

...Not only will you get your tenth lesson <u>free</u> when you book 10 lessons, but we'll also give you our award-winning 'map' Mind Alertness Programme worth £18.99 <u>free</u>.

'map' is an interactive CD package that gives you a better chance of passing your Practical Test by improving a range of mental abilities, such as judging speed and distances.

Plus, you'll also get:

– free Theory Test and Hazard Perception training

– free RAC Roadside cover when you pass

... And you can top it all off by training in one of our air-conditioned Vauxhall Corsas or Astras

So, what are you waiting for, book now

## 08457 276 276
## www.bsm.co.uk
Quote VTTQC

✂ - - - - - - - - - - - - - - - - - - - - - - - - - - - - - - - - - - - - - - - - - - - - - - - - - - - -

## Free driving lesson plus free 'map' CD-ROM
### Simply present the completed coupon to your Instructor before your first lesson.

| | BSM Centre use only |
|---|---|
| Name _____ | Centre code _____ |
| Address _____ | PEP No. _____ |
| _____ | Value _____ |
| Postcode _____ | Car No. _____ |
| Date _____ Mobile _____ | Date _____ |
| | Code VTTQC _____ |

Terms and conditions: The offer is for your tenth lesson free, a copy of BSM's 'map' CD-ROM (normally worth £18.99) and free RAC Roadside cover (which you must activate when you pass your Practical Test) when you block book and pay for 10 lessons. Offer is valid until 30/06/05. Lesson duration is 60 minutes (normally booked in two hour blocks). Only one coupon per learner. Offer cannot be used in conjunction with any other offer and cannot be used by any individual currently taking lessons with a BSM Instructor. Offer only available on production of a valid and completed coupon at your first lesson. Original coupons must be presented – no photocopies accepted. Offer subject to availability. Discount and free CD-ROM not available when purchasing gift vouchers and not transferable for cash or gift vouchers. Promoter: British School of Motoring Limited (company no. 291902). Registered office: 1 Forest Road, Feltham, Middlesex TW13 7RR. Calls may be monitored and recorded.

# Theory Test Questions for Car Drivers

2004–2005

All the questions and answers valid
for tests taken after July 1, 2003

Published by BSM in association with
Virgin Publishing

First published in the UK in 2003 by
The British School of Motoring Ltd
1 Forest Road
Feltham
Middlesex
TW13 7RR

Copyright © 2003 The British School of Motoring Ltd

First reprint 2004

This book is based on material supplied by the Driving Standards Agency
and contains Crown Copyright material produced under licence from
the Controller of HMSO and the Driving Standards Agency. All rights reserved.

No part of this product may be reproduced, stored in a retrieval system or transmitted,
in any form or by any means; electronic, electrostatic, internet, magnetic tape,
mechanical, photocopying, recording, w.w.w. or otherwise, without permission in
writing from the publisher, DSA and HMSO's copyright unit.

Graphic design of all illustrations contained in the Theory Test
is copyright of The Stationery Office.

ISBN 0 7535 0875 3

Design, typesetting and reprographics by Thalamus Publishing

Printed in Italy

# Contents

# Foreword

Driving is an enjoyable and valuable life skill which is why every year about a million new learners take to the road, each one of them with one clear aim. This aim is almost certainly the same as yours – to gain their full licence.

There is no substitute for practical experience when learning to drive. The best way to gain this is by taking lessons with a good professional instructor who uses the most up-to-date teaching techniques in a modern, dual-controlled car. However, it has always been equally important to prepare for your driving lessons and, since the introduction of the Theory Test, this is doubly true.

Theory Test Questions for Car Drivers contains the revised set (valid for tests after July 1, 2003) of official Driving Standards Agency questions which are currently published and which may be included in the actual examination.

This book is an ideal study aid which allows you to test and revise your knowledge. It has been designed for use in conjunction with its companion volumes, Pass Your Driving Theory Test, Pass Your Driving Test and Practice Sessions.

Theory Test Questions for Car Drivers allows you to check your level of knowledge by presenting you with real examination questions. The questions are set out under topic headings, and as you work through each section you will prove to yourself that you not only understand what you have learnt, but can demonstrate this by answering the question correctly.

In doing so, you will gradually boost your confidence and thereby recognise when you are ready to take and pass the Theory Test.

Your instructor will help you to plan your studies and ensure that you fully understand why the knowledge you acquire is essential to keep you safe on the road, as well as to take you past that first all important hurdle of passing the Theory Test.

There are no short cuts to becoming a safe and competent motorist, but that does not mean that you cannot enjoy yourself while learning.

Theory Test Questions for Car Drivers and its companion volumes will, I hope, bring the Theory Test alive and make it relevant, and at the same time it should also help you develop your driving skills.

In 90 years of teaching people to drive, BSM instructors have helped millions of people pass their driving tests. In my view, Theory Test Questions for Car Drivers completes the best set of books available to help you make the most of

your lessons and ensure that you prepare for both the theory and practical parts of your driving test in a structured and positive way.

Keith Cameron
Road Safety Adviser

Keith Cameron is one of Britain's leading authorities on motoring and driver education. He has held a number of senior positions within the Department of Transport, including Chief Driving Examiner where he had responsibility for all UK driving tests.

# Introduction

Some learners view the Theory Test only as an irrelevant exam which you have to do on the way to getting a full licence. However, learning answers to questions without understanding the meaning will not improve your skills and is not the best way to pass your Driving Theory Test. You need to think clearly about what answer the question is looking for and then make sure that you understand how that answer can assist your practical driving skills. The companion publication to this book, BSM's Pass Your Driving Theory Test, has been specially written to help you understand the questions and answers, rather than just knowing them.

Remember, when you actually sit the Theory Test you will have plenty of time to read the questions thoroughly. Make sure you understand what is being asked. Don't rush or panic; instead think carefully about each suggested answer. Invariably, if you have put the time and effort into studying, the correct answer or answers should be more than apparent. If you have queries or areas that you do not understand, you should ask your instructor.

This book contains all 894 of the official multiple-choice questions that make up the current DSA question bank. In your

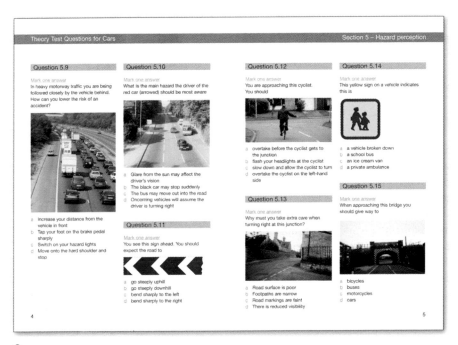

Theory Test, you are asked 35 of these questions. You need to provide the correct answers to at least 30 in order to pass the multiple-choice element of the Theory Test. At the Test Centre, you sit at a computer and the questions appear on the computer screen. You select your answers by simply touching the screen. This touch-screen system has been carefully designed to make it easy to use.

The second element of the Theory Test is Hazard Perception. In this part of the Test, you are shown video footage of real road situations and you are expected to quickly identify developing hazards. Whereas the multiple-choice section of the Test assesses your knowledge and understanding, the Hazard Perception section tests your awareness and skills.

Therefore, you need to prepare for this part of the Test in a different way. BSM has several publications and computer-based training aids which have been specially designed to help with your preparation; for details of these, or for more information about the Hazard Perception test, visit www.bsm.co.uk or call us on 08457 276276. Remember that you need to pass Hazard Perception at the same sitting as the multiple-choice section of the Test, otherwise you need to take the whole Test again.

The important point about the Theory Test is that it is not an irrelevant exam. All parts of the Test are interconnected with the practical elements of your driver training and all contribute to making you a better, safer driver. Proper study and understanding of the subjects covered by both parts of the Theory Test will also be a great help in securing a pass on the Practical Test.

Note: Questions marked NI Exempt are not part of the Driving Theory Test in Northern Ireland

# Theory Test Questions for Car Drivers

2004–2005

## Section 1    Alertness

## Question 1.1

Mark one answer
Before you make a U-turn in the road, you should

a give an arm signal as well as using your indicators
b signal so that other drivers can slow down for you
c look over your shoulder for a final check
d select a higher gear than normal

## Question 1.2

Mark three answers
As you approach this bridge you should

a move into the middle of the road to get a better view
b slow down
c get over the bridge as quickly as possible
d consider using your horn
e find another route
f beware of pedestrians

## Question 1.3

Mark one answer
When following a large vehicle you should keep well back because

a it allows you to corner more quickly
b it helps the large vehicle to stop more easily
c it allows the driver to see you in the mirrors
d it helps you to keep out of the wind

## Question 1.4

Mark one answer
In which of these situations should you avoid overtaking?

a Just after a bend
b In a one-way street
c On a 30mph road
d Approaching a dip in the road

## Question 1.5

Mark one answer
This road marking warns

a  drivers to use the hard shoulder
b  overtaking drivers there is a bend to the left
c  overtaking drivers to move back to the left
d  drivers that it is safe to overtake

## Question 1.6

Mark one answer
Your mobile phone rings while you are travelling. You should

a  stop immediately
b  answer it immediately
c  pull up in a suitable place
d  pull up at the nearest kerb

## Question 1.7

Mark one answer
Why are these yellow lines painted across the road?

a  To help you choose the correct lane
b  To help you keep the correct separation distance
c  To make you aware of your speed
d  To tell you the distance to the roundabout

## Question 1.8

Mark one answer
You are approaching traffic lights that have been on green for some time. You should

a  accelerate hard
b  maintain your speed
c  be ready to stop
d  brake hard

## Question 1.9

Mark one answer
Which of the following should you do before stopping?

a  Sound the horn
b  Use the mirrors
c  Select a higher gear
d  Flash your headlights

## Question 1.10

Mark one answer
As a driver what does the term 'Blind Spot' mean?

a  An area covered by your right-hand mirror
b  An area not covered by your headlamps
c  An area covered by your left-hand mirror
d  An area not seen in your mirrors

## Question 1.11

Mark two answers
Objects hanging from your interior mirror may

a  restrict your view
b  improve your driving
c  distract your attention
d  help your concentration

## Question 1.12

Mark four answers
Which of the following may cause loss of concentration on a long journey?

a  Loud music
b  Arguing with a passenger
c  Using a mobile phone
d  Putting in a cassette tape
e  Stopping regularly to rest
f  Pulling up to tune the radio

## Question 1.13

Mark two answers
On a long motorway journey boredom can cause you to feel sleepy. You should

a  leave the motorway and find a safe place to stop
b  keep looking around at the surrounding landscape
c  drive faster to complete your journey sooner
d  ensure a supply of fresh air into your vehicle
e  stop on the hard shoulder for a rest

## Question 1.14

Mark two answers
You are driving at dusk. You should switch your lights on

a   even when street lights are not lit
b   so others can see you
c   only when others have done so
d   only when street lights are lit

## Question 1.15

Mark two answers
You are most likely to lose concentration when driving if you

a   use a mobile phone
b   listen to very loud music
c   switch on the heated rear window
d   look at the door mirrors

## Question 1.16

Mark four answers
Which FOUR are most likely to cause you to lose concentration while you are driving?

a   Using a mobile phone
b   Talking into a microphone
c   Tuning your car radio
d   Looking at a map
e   Checking the mirrors
f   Using the demisters

## Question 1.17

Mark one answer
You should not use a mobile phone whilst driving

a   until you are satisfied that no other traffic is near
b   unless you are able to drive one-handed
c   because it might distract your attention from the road ahead
d   because reception is poor when the engine is running

## Question 1.18

Mark one answer
Your vehicle is fitted with a hands-free phone system. Using this equipment while driving

a   is quite safe as long as you slow down
b   could distract your attention from the road
c   is recommended by The Highway Code
d   could be very good for road safety

## Question 1.19

Mark one answer
Using a hands-free phone is likely to

a   improve your safety
b   increase your concentration
c   reduce your view
d   divert your attention

## Question 1.20

Mark one answer
You should ONLY use a mobile phone when

a   receiving a call
b   suitably parked
c   driving at less than 30mph
d   driving an automatic vehicle

## Question 1.21

Mark one answer
Using a mobile phone while you are driving

a   is acceptable in a vehicle with power steering
b   will reduce your field of vision
c   could distract your attention from the road
d   will affect your vehicle's electronic systems

## Question 1.22

Mark one answer
What is the safest way to use a mobile phone in your vehicle?

a   Use hands-free equipment
b   Find a suitable place to stop
c   Drive slowly on a quiet road
d   Direct your call through the operator

## Question 1.23

Mark one answer
You are driving on a wet road. You have to stop your vehicle in an emergency. You should

a   apply the handbrake and footbrake together
b   keep both hands on the wheel
c   select reverse gear
d   give an arm signal

## Question 1.24

Mark three answers
When you are moving off from behind a parked car you should

a   look round before you move off
b   use all the mirrors on the vehicle
c   look round after moving off
d   use the exterior mirrors only
e   give a signal if necessary
f   give a signal after moving off

## Question 1.25

Mark one answer

You are travelling along this narrow country road. When passing the cyclist you should go

a  slowly, sounding the horn as you pass

b  quickly, leaving plenty of room

c  slowly, leaving plenty of room

d  quickly, sounding the horn as you pass

## Question 1.26

Mark one answer

Your vehicle is fitted with a hand-held telephone. To use the telephone you should

a  reduce your speed

b  find a safe place to stop

c  steer the vehicle with one hand

d  be particularly careful at junctions

## Question 1.27

Mark one answer

To answer a call on your mobile phone while travelling you should

a  reduce your speed wherever you are

b  stop in a proper and convenient place

c  keep the call time to a minimum

d  slow down and allow others to overtake

## Question 1.28 NI Exempt

Mark one answer

Your mobile phone rings while you are on the motorway. Before answering you should

a  reduce your speed to 50mph

b  pull up on the hard shoulder

c  move into the left-hand lane

d  stop in a safe place

## Question 1.29

Mark one answer

You are turning right onto a dual carriageway. What should you do before emerging?

a  Stop, apply the handbrake and then select a low gear
b  Position your vehicle well to the left of the side road
c  Check that the central reserve is wide enough for your vehicle
d  Make sure that you leave enough room for a following vehicle

## Question 1.30

Mark one answer

You lose your way on a busy road. What is the best action to take?

a  Stop at traffic lights and ask pedestrians
b  Shout to other drivers to ask them the way
c  Turn into a side road, stop and check a map
d  Check a map, and keep going with the traffic flow

## Question 1.31

Mark one answer

You are waiting to emerge from a junction. The screen pillar is restricting your view. What should you be particularly aware of?

a  Lorries
b  Buses
c  Motorcyclists
d  Coaches

## Question 1.32

Mark one answer

When emerging from junctions which is most likely to obstruct your view?

a  Windscreen pillars
b  Steering wheel
c  Interior mirror
d  Windscreen wipers

## Question 1.33

Mark one answer

Windscreen pillars can obstruct your view. You should take particular care when

a driving on a motorway
b driving on a dual carriageway
c approaching a one-way street
d approaching bends and junctions

## Question 1.34

Mark one answer

You cannot see clearly behind when reversing. What should you do?

a Open your window to look behind
b Open the door and look behind
c Look in the nearside mirror
d Ask someone to guide you

## Answers and explanations

1.1   c You should always check your blind spot just before moving off or starting a manoeuvre.
1.2   b, d, f
1.3   c
1.4   d
1.5   c
1.6   c Answering a mobile phone while driving might distract your attention. You should pull up first.
1.7   c
1.8   c Be ready to stop because the traffic lights may change colour before you pass them.
1.9   b
1.10   d
1.11   a, c
1.12   a, b, c, d
1.13   a, d
1.14   a, b
1.15   a, b
1.16   a, b, c, d
1.17   c
1.18   b
1.19   d You are not allowed to use a hand-held mobile phone whilst driving. Even a hands-free system can distract your attention from the road.
1.20   b
1.21   c
1.22   b
1.23   b This helps you maintain control of your car.
1.24   a, b, e
1.25   c

1.26  b You must not use a hand-held telephone while you are driving.

1.27  b If it's a hand-held phone you must pull up before answering. If it's hands-free it is still advisable to stop.

1.28  d

1.29  c This is because if there is no traffic coming from the right, but there is traffic comng from the left, you may wait in the central reservation provided that it's wide enough for your vehicle.

1.30  c Because the road is busy it would be better to leave the road before stopping to check the map.

1.31  c Because they are small enough to be hidden by the pillar.

1.32  a

1.33  d

1.34  d If you cannot see properly, you need to get someone to help.

# Theory Test Questions for Car Drivers

2004–2005

Section 2    Attitudes to other road users

## Question 2.1

Mark one answer

At a pelican crossing the flashing amber light means you MUST

a  stop and wait for the green light
b  stop and wait for the red light
c  give way to pedestrians waiting to cross
d  give way to pedestrians already on the crossing

## Question 2.2

Mark one answer

You should never wave people across at pedestrian crossings because

a  there may be another vehicle coming
b  they may not be looking
c  it is safer for you to carry on
d  they may not be ready to cross

## Question 2.3

Mark one answer

At a puffin crossing what colour follows the green signal?

a  Steady red
b  Flashing amber
c  Steady amber
d  Flashing green

## Question 2.4

Mark one answer

You could use the 'Two-Second Rule'

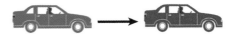

a  before restarting the engine after it has stalled
b  to keep a safe gap from the vehicle in front
c  before using the 'Mirror-Signal-Manoeuvre' routine
d  when emerging on wet roads

## Question 2.5

Mark one answer

'Tailgating' means

a  using the rear door of a hatchback car
b  reversing into a parking space
c  following another vehicle too closely
d  driving with rear fog lights on

## Question 2.6

Mark one answer

A long, heavily-laden lorry is taking a long time to overtake you. What should you do?

a  Speed up
b  Slow down
c  Hold your speed
d  Change direction

## Question 2.7

Mark one answer

Following this vehicle too closely is unwise because

a  your brakes will overheat
b  your view ahead is increased
c  your engine will overheat
d  your view ahead is reduced

## Question 2.8

Mark one answer

You are following a vehicle on a wet road. You should leave a time gap of at least

a  one second
b  two seconds
c  three seconds
d  four seconds

## Question 2.9

Mark one answer

You are in a line of traffic. The driver behind you is following very closely. What action should you take?

a  Ignore the following driver and continue to drive within the speed limit
b  Slow down, gradually increasing the gap between you and the vehicle in front
c  Signal left and wave the following driver past
d  Move over to a position just left of the centre line of the road

## Question 2.10

Mark three answers

Which of the following vehicles will use blue flashing beacons?

a  Motorway maintenance
b  Bomb disposal
c  Blood transfusion
d  Police patrol
e  Breakdown recovery

23

## Question 2.11

<u>Mark three answers</u>
Which THREE of these emergency services might have blue flashing beacons?

a  Coastguard
b  Bomb disposal
c  Gritting lorries
d  Animal ambulances
e  Mountain rescue
f  Doctors' cars

## Question 2.12

<u>Mark one answer</u>
When being followed by an ambulance showing a flashing blue beacon you should

a  pull over as soon as safely possible to let it pass
b  accelerate hard to get away from it
c  maintain your speed and course
d  brake harshly and immediately stop in the road

## Question 2.13

<u>Mark one answer</u>
What type of emergency vehicle is fitted with a green flashing beacon?

a  Fire engine
b  Road gritter
c  Ambulance
d  Doctor's car

## Question 2.14

<u>Mark one answer</u>
A flashing green beacon on a vehicle means

a  police on non-urgent duties
b  doctor on an emergency call
c  road safety patrol operating
d  gritting in progress

## Question 2.15

<u>Mark one answer</u>
A vehicle has a flashing green beacon. What does this mean?

a  A doctor is answering an emergency call
b  The vehicle is slow-moving
c  It is a motorway police patrol vehicle
d  A vehicle is carrying hazardous chemicals

## Question 2.16

<u>Mark one answer</u>
Diamond-shaped signs give instructions to

a  tram drivers
b  bus drivers
c  lorry drivers
d  taxi drivers

## Question 2.17

Mark one answer
On a road where trams operate, which of these vehicles will be most at risk from the tram rails?

a Cars
b Cycles
c Buses
d Lorries

## Question 2.18

Mark one answer
What should you use your horn for?

a To alert others to your presence
b To allow you right of way
c To greet other road users
d To signal your annoyance

## Question 2.19

Mark one answer
You are in a one-way street and want to turn right. You should position yourself

a in the right-hand lane
b in the left-hand lane
c in either lane, depending on the traffic
d just left of the centre line

## Question 2.20

Mark one answer
You wish to turn right ahead. Why should you take up the correct position in good time?

a To allow other drivers to pull out in front of you
b To give a better view into the road that you're joining
c To help other road users know what you intend to do
d To allow drivers to pass you on the right

## Question 2.21

Mark one answer
At which type of crossing are cyclists allowed to ride across with pedestrians?

a Toucan
b Puffin
c Pelican
d Zebra

## Question 2.22

Mark one answer

A bus is stopped at a bus stop ahead of you. Its right-hand indicator is flashing. You should

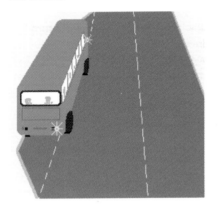

a   flash your headlights and slow down
b   slow down and give way if it is safe to do so
c   sound your horn and keep going
d   slow down and then sound your horn

## Question 2.23

Mark one answer

You are travelling at the legal speed limit. A vehicle comes up quickly behind, flashing its headlights. You should

a   accelerate to make a gap behind you
b   touch the brakes sharply to show your brake lights
c   maintain your speed to prevent the vehicle from overtaking
d   allow the vehicle to overtake

## Question 2.24

Mark one answer

You should ONLY flash your headlights to other road users

a   to show that you are giving way
b   to show that you are about to turn
c   to tell them that you have right of way
d   to let them know that you are there

## Question 2.25

Mark one answer

You are approaching an unmarked crossroads. How should you deal with this type of junction?

a   Accelerate and keep to the middle
b   Slow down and keep to the right
c   Accelerate looking to the left
d   Slow down and look both ways

## Question 2.26

Mark one answer

You are approaching a pelican crossing. The amber light is flashing. You must

a   give way to pedestrians who are crossing
b   encourage pedestrians to cross
c   not move until the green light appears
d   stop even if the crossing is clear

## Question 2.27

Mark one answer

At puffin crossings which light will not show to a driver?

a Flashing amber
b Red
c Steady amber
d Green

## Question 2.28

Mark one answer

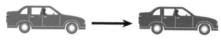

A two-second gap between yourself and the car in front is sufficient when conditions are
a wet
b good
c damp
d foggy

## Question 2.29

Mark one answer

You are driving on a clear night. There is a steady stream of oncoming traffic. The national speed limit applies. Which lights should you use?

a Full beam headlights
b Sidelights
c Dipped headlights
d Fog lights

## Question 2.30

Mark one answer

You are driving behind a large goods vehicle. It signals left but steers to the right. You should

a slow down and let the vehicle turn
b drive on, keeping to the left
c overtake on the right of it
d hold your speed and sound your horn

## Question 2.31

Mark one answer

You are driving along this road. The red van cuts in close in front of you. What should you do?

a Accelerate to get closer to the red van
b Give a long blast on the horn
c Drop back to leave the correct separation distance
d Flash your headlights several times

## Question 2.32

Mark one answer

You are waiting in a traffic queue at night. To avoid dazzling following drivers you should

a apply the handbrake only
b apply the footbrake only
c switch off your headlights
d use both the handbrake and footbrake

## Question 2.33

Mark one answer

You are driving in traffic at the speed limit for the road. The driver behind is trying to overtake. You should

a move closer to the car ahead, so the driver behind has no room to overtake
b wave the driver behind to overtake when it is safe
c keep a steady course and allow the driver behind to overtake
d accelerate to get away from the driver behind

## Question 2.34

Mark one answer

You are driving at night on an unlit road following a slower-moving vehicle. You should

a flash your headlights
b use dipped beam headlights
c switch off your headlights
d use full beam headlights

## Question 2.35

Mark one answer

A bus lane on your left shows no times of operation. This means it is

a not in operation at all
b only in operation at peak times
c in operation 24 hours a day
d only in operation in daylight hours

## Question 2.36

Mark two answers

You are driving along a country road. A horse and rider are approaching. What should you do?

a  Increase your speed
b  Sound your horn
c  Flash your headlights
d  Drive slowly past
e  Give plenty of room
f  Rev your engine

## Question 2.37

Mark one answer

A person herding sheep asks you to stop. You should

a  ignore them as they have no authority
b  stop and switch off your engine
c  continue on but drive slowly
d  try and get past quickly

## Question 2.38

Mark one answer

When overtaking a horse and rider you should

a  sound your horn as a warning
b  go past as quickly as possible
c  flash your headlights as a warning
d  go past slowly and carefully

## Question 2.39

Mark one answer

You are approaching a zebra crossing. Pedestrians are waiting to cross. You should

a  give way to the elderly and infirm only
b  slow down and prepare to stop
c  use your headlights to indicate they can cross
d  wave at them to cross the road

## Question 2.40

Mark one answer

You are driving a slow-moving vehicle on a narrow, winding road. You should

a  keep well out to stop vehicles overtaking dangerously
b  wave following vehicles past you if you think they can overtake quickly
c  pull in safely when you can, to let following vehicles overtake
d  give a left signal when it is safe for vehicles to overtake you

## Question 2.41

Mark one answer

You are driving a slow-moving vehicle on a narrow road. When traffic wishes to overtake you should

a  take no action
b  put your hazard warning lights on
c  stop immediately and wave it on
d  pull in safely as soon as you can do so

## Question 2.42

Mark one answer

You are driving a slow-moving vehicle on a narrow, winding road. In order to let other vehicles overtake you should

a  wave to them to pass
b  pull in when you can
c  show a left turn signal
d  keep left and hold your speed

## Question 2.43

Mark one answer

A vehicle pulls out in front of you at a junction. What should you do?

a  Swerve past it and sound your horn
b  Flash your headlights and drive up close behind
c  Slow down and be ready to stop
d  Accelerate past it immediately

## Question 2.44

Mark one answer

You stop for pedestrians waiting to cross at a zebra crossing. They do not start to cross. What should you do?

a  Be patient and wait
b  Sound your horn
c  Carry on
d  Wave them to cross

## Question 2.45

Mark one answer

You are following this lorry. You should keep well back from it to

a  give you a good view of the road ahead
b  stop following traffic from rushing through the junction
c  prevent traffic behind you from overtaking
d  allow you to hurry through the traffic lights if they change

## Question 2.46

Mark one answer

You are approaching a red light at a puffin crossing. Pedestrians are on the crossing. The red light will stay on until

a  you start to edge forward on to the crossing
b  the pedestrians have reached a safe position
c  the pedestrians are clear of the front of your vehicle
d  a driver from the opposite direction reaches the crossing

## Question 2.47

Mark one answer

Which instrument panel warning light would show that headlights are on full beam ?

   a       b       c       d

## Answers and explanations

2.1   d
2.2   a
2.3   c
2.4   b A two-second time gap from the vehicle in front provides a safe gap in good conditions.

2.5   c
2.6   b By slowing down, you allow the lorry to get past, which is the only safe option.
2.7   d If you hang back you will have a much better view of the road ahead.
2.8   d In good conditions you should allow two seconds but on a wet road you double this to four.
2.9   b By increasing the gap between you and the vehicle in front, you give yourself and the driver behind more room to stop should you need it.
2.10  b, c, d
2.11  a, b, e
2.12  a
2.13  d Doctors on emergency call may display a flashing green beacon. Slow-moving vehicles have amber flashing beacons. Police, fire and ambulance service vehicles have blue flashing beacons.
2.14  b
2.15  a
2.16  a
2.17  b
2.18  a

2.19   a To turn right from a one-way
          street you normally position
          yourself in the right-hand lane.
2.20   c The position of your car
          helps signal your intentions
          to other drivers.
2.21   a
2.22   b
2.23   d This is your only safe option.
2.24   d You should only flash your
          headlights to warn other road
          users that you are there.
2.25   d Because no one has priority.
2.26   a You must give way to
          pedestrians already on the
          crossing but may drive on if the
          crossing is clear.
2.27   a
2.28   b
2.29   c
2.30   a
2.31   c
2.32   a Using the footbrake would
          activate your brake lights and
          might dazzle following drivers.
2.33   c
2.34   b
2.35   c
2.36   d, e
2.37   b
2.38   d
2.39   b
2.40   c 'a' and 'b' are dangerous and 'd'
          is confusing. Other drivers might
          think you are stopping or turning
          left.
2.41   d
2.42   b

2.43   c This is the only safe thing to do.
          The other answers are the
          actions of an aggressive driver.
2.44   a
2.45   a The nearer you are to a lorry,
          the less you can see ahead.
2.46   b
2.47   a

# Theory Test Questions for Car Drivers

2004–2005

Section 3    Vehicle defects, safety equipment and the environment

## Question 3.1

Mark one answer

Which of these, if allowed to get low, could cause an accident?

a  Antifreeze level
b  Brake fluid level
c  Battery water level
d  Radiator coolant level

## Question 3.2

Mark two answers

Which TWO are badly affected if the tyres are under-inflated?

a  Braking
b  Steering
c  Changing gear
d  Parking

## Question 3.3

Mark three answers

The pictured vehicle is 'environmentally friendly' because it

a  reduces noise pollution
b  uses diesel fuel
c  uses electricity
d  uses unleaded fuel
e  reduces parking spaces
f  reduces town traffic

## Question 3.4

Mark three answers

Excessive or uneven tyre wear can be caused by faults in which THREE?

a  The gearbox
b  The braking system
c  The accelerator
d  The exhaust system
e  Wheel alignment
f  The suspension

## Question 3.5

Mark one answer

You must NOT sound your horn

a  between 10 pm and 6 am in a built-up area
b  at any time in a built-up area
c  between 11.30 pm and 7 am in a built-up area
d  between 11.30 pm and 6 am on any road

## Question 3.6

Mark three answers

Motor vehicles can harm the environment. This has resulted in

a  air pollution
b  damage to buildings
c  reduced health risks
d  improved public transport
e  less use of electrical vehicles
f  using up natural resources

## Question 3.7

Mark one answer

Supertrams or Light Rapid Transit (LRT) systems are environmentally friendly because

a  they use diesel power
b  they use quieter roads
c  they use electric power
d  they do not operate during rush hour

## Question 3.8

Mark one answer

'Red routes' in major cities have been introduced to

a  raise the speed limits
b  help the traffic flow
c  provide better parking
d  allow lorries to load more freely

## Question 3.9

Mark one answer

In some narrow, residential streets you will find a speed limit of

a  20mph
b  25mph
c  35mph
d  40mph

## Question 3.10

Mark one answer

Road humps, chicanes, and narrowings are

a  always at major road works
b  used to increase traffic speed
c  at toll-bridge approaches only
d  traffic-calming measures

## Question 3.11

Mark one answer

The purpose of a catalytic converter is to reduce

a  fuel consumption
b  the risk of fire
c  toxic exhaust gases
d  engine wear

## Question 3.12

Mark one answer

Catalytic converters are fitted to make the

a  engine produce more power
b  exhaust system easier to replace
c  engine run quietly
d  exhaust fumes cleaner

## Question 3.13

Mark one answer

It is essential that tyre pressures are checked regularly. When should this be done?

a  After any lengthy journey
b  After travelling at high speed
c  When tyres are hot
d  When tyres are cold

## Question 3.14

Mark one answer

When should you NOT use your horn in a built-up area?

a  Between 8 pm and 8 am
b  Between 9 pm and dawn
c  Between dusk and 8 am
d  Between 11.30 pm and 7 am

## Question 3.15

Mark one answer

You will use more fuel if your tyres are

a  under-inflated
b  of different makes
c  over-inflated
d  new and hardly used

## Question 3.16

Mark two answers

How should you dispose of a used battery?

a  Take it to a local authority site
b  Put it in the dustbin
c  Break it up into pieces
d  Leave it on waste land
e  Take it to a garage
f  Burn it on a fire

## Question 3.17

Mark one answer

What is most likely to cause high fuel consumption?

a  Poor steering control
b  Accelerating around bends
c  Staying in high gears
d  Harsh braking and accelerating

## Question 3.18

Mark one answer

The fluid level in your battery is low. What should you top it up with?

a  Battery acid
b  Distilled water
c  Engine oil
d  Engine coolant

## Question 3.19

Mark one answer

You need to top up your battery. What level should you fill to?

a  The top of the battery
b  Half-way up the battery
c  Just below the cell plates
d  Just above the cell plates

## Question 3.20

Mark one answer

You have too much oil in your engine. What could this cause?

a  Low oil pressure
b  Engine overheating
c  Chain wear
d  Oil leaks

## Question 3.21

Mark one answer

You are parking on a two-way road at night. The speed limit is 40mph. You should park on the

a  left with parking lights on
b  left with no lights on
c  right with parking lights on
d  right with dipped headlights on

## Question 3.22

Mark one answer

You are parked on the road at night. Where must you use parking lights?

a  Where there are continuous white lines in the middle of the road
b  Where the speed limit exceeds 30mph
c  Where you are facing oncoming traffic
d  Where you are near a bus stop

## Question 3.23

Mark four answers

Which FOUR of these MUST be in good working order for your car to be roadworthy?

a  Temperature gauge
b  Speedometer
c  Windscreen washers
d  Windscreen wiper
e  Oil warning light
f  Horn

## Question 3.24

Mark one answer

New petrol-engined cars must be fitted with catalytic converters. The reason for this is to

a  control exhaust noise levels
b  prolong the life of the exhaust system
c  allow the exhaust system to be recycled
d  reduce harmful exhaust emissions

## Question 3.25

Mark one answer

What can cause heavy steering?

a  Driving on ice
b  Badly worn brakes
c  Over-inflated tyres
d  Under-inflated tyres

## Question 3.26

Mark two answers

Driving with under-inflated tyres can affect

a  engine temperature
b  fuel consumption
c  braking
d  oil pressure

## Question 3.27

Mark two answers

Excessive or uneven tyre wear can be caused by faults in the

a  gearbox
b  braking system
c  suspension
d  exhaust system

## Question 3.28

Mark one answer

The main cause of brake fade is

a  the brakes overheating
b  air in the brake fluid
c  oil on the brakes
d  the brakes out of adjustment

## Question 3.29

Mark one answer

Your anti-lock brakes warning light stays on. You should

a  check the brake fluid level
b  check the footbrake free play
c  check that the handbrake is released
d  have the brakes checked immediately

## Question 3.30

Mark one answer

What does this instrument panel light mean when lit?

a Gear lever in park
b Gear lever in neutral
c Handbrake on
d Handbrake off

## Question 3.31

Mark one answer

While driving, this warning light on your dashboard comes on. It means

a a fault in the braking system
b the engine oil is low
c a rear light has failed
d your seat belt is not fastened

## Question 3.32

Mark one answer

It is important to wear suitable shoes when you are driving. Why is this?

a To prevent wear on the pedals
b To maintain control of the pedals
c To enable you to adjust your seat
d To enable you to walk for assistance if you break down

## Question 3.33

Mark one answer

A properly-adjusted head restraint will

a make you more comfortable
b help you to avoid neck injury
c help you to relax
d help you to maintain your driving position

## Question 3.34

Mark one answer

What will reduce the risk of neck injury resulting from a collision?

a An air-sprung seat
b Anti-lock brakes
c A collapsible steering wheel
d A properly-adjusted head restraint

## Question 3.35

Mark one answer

You are driving a friend's children home from school. They are both under 14 years old. Who is responsible for making sure they wear a seat belt?

a   An adult passenger
b   The children
c   You, the driver
d   Your friend

## Question 3.36

Mark one answer

Car passengers MUST wear a seat belt if one is available, unless they are

a   under 14 years old
b   under 1.5 metres (5 feet) in height
c   sitting in the rear seat
d   exempt for medical reasons

## Question 3.37

Mark one answer

You are testing your suspension. You notice that your vehicle keeps bouncing when you press down on the front wing. What does this mean?

a   Worn tyres
b   Tyres under-inflated
c   Steering wheel not located centrally
d   Worn shock absorbers

## Question 3.38

Mark one answer

A roof rack fitted to your car will

a   reduce fuel consumption
b   improve the road handling
c   make your car go faster
d   increase fuel consumption

## Question 3.39

Mark one answer

It is illegal to drive with tyres that

a   have been bought second-hand
b   have a large deep cut in the side wall
c   are of different makes
d   are of different tread patterns

## Question 3.40

Mark one answer

The legal minimum depth of tread for car tyres over three quarters of the breadth is

a   1 mm
b   1.6 mm
c   2.5 mm
d   4 mm

## Question 3.41

Mark one answer

You are carrying two 13-year-old children and their parents in your car. Who is responsible for seeing that the children wear seat belts?

a The children's parents
b You, the driver
c The front-seat passenger
d The children

## Question 3.42

Mark one answer

When a roof rack is not in use it should be removed. Why is this?

a It will affect the suspension
b It is illegal
c It will affect your braking
d It will waste fuel

## Question 3.43

Mark two answers

You have a loose filler cap on your diesel fuel tank. This will

a waste fuel and money
b make roads slippery for other road users
c improve your vehicles fuel consumption
d increase the level of exhaust emissions

## Question 3.44

Mark three answers

How can you, as a driver, help the environment?

a By reducing your speed
b By gentle acceleration
c By using leaded fuel
d By driving faster
e By harsh acceleration
f By servicing your vehicle properly

## Question 3.45

Mark three answers

To help the environment, you can avoid wasting fuel by

a having your vehicle properly serviced
b making sure your tyres are correctly inflated
c not over-revving in the lower gears
d driving at higher speeds where possible
e keeping an empty roof rack properly fitted
f servicing your vehicle less regularly

41

## Question 3.46

Mark three answers
To reduce the volume of traffic on the roads you could

a   use public transport more often
b   share a car when possible
c   walk or cycle on short journeys
d   travel by car at all times
e   use a car with a smaller engine
f   drive in a bus lane

## Question 3.47

Mark three answers
Which THREE of the following are most likely to waste fuel?

a   Reducing your speed
b   Carrying unnecessary weight
c   Using the wrong grade of fuel
d   Under-inflated tyres
e   Using different brands of fuel
f   A fitted, empty roof rack

## Question 3.48

Mark one answer
To avoid spillage after refuelling, you should make sure that

a   your tank is only 3/4 full
b   you have used a locking filler cap
c   you check your fuel gauge is working
d   your filler cap is securely fastened

## Question 3.49

Mark three answers
Which THREE things can you, as a road user, do to help the environment?

a   Cycle when possible
b   Drive on under-inflated tyres
c   Use the choke for as long as possible on a cold engine
d   Have your vehicle properly tuned and serviced
e   Watch the traffic and plan ahead
f   Brake as late as possible without skidding

## Question 3.50

Mark three answers
As a driver you can cause MORE damage to the environment by

a   choosing a fuel efficient vehicle
b   making a lot of short journeys
c   driving in as high a gear as possible
d   accelerating as quickly as possible
e   having your vehicle regularly serviced
f   using leaded fuel

## Question 3.51

Mark one answer

Extra care should be taken when refuelling, because diesel fuel when spilt is

a   sticky
b   odourless
c   clear
d   slippery

## Question 3.52

Mark one answer

To help protect the environment you should NOT

a   remove your roof rack when unloaded
b   use your car for very short journeys
c   walk, cycle, or use public transport
d   empty the boot of unnecessary weight

## Question 3.53

Mark three answers

Which THREE does the law require you to keep in good condition?

a   Gears
b   Transmission
c   Headlights
d   Windscreen
e   Seat belts

## Question 3.54

Mark one answer

Driving at 70mph uses more fuel than driving at 50mph by up to

a   10%
b   30%
c   75%
d   100%

## Question 3.55

Mark one answer

Your vehicle pulls to one side when braking. You should

a   change the tyres around
b   consult your garage as soon as possible
c   pump the pedal when braking
d   use your handbrake at the same time

## Question 3.56

Mark one answer

As a driver you can help reduce pollution levels in town centres by

a   driving more quickly
b   using leaded fuel
c   walking or cycling
d   driving short journeys

## Question 3.57

Mark one answer

Unbalanced wheels on a car may cause

a   the steering to pull to one side
b   the steering to vibrate
c   the brakes to fail
d   the tyres to deflate

## Question 3.58

Mark two answers

Turning the steering wheel while your car is stationary can cause damage to the

a   gearbox
b   engine
c   brakes
d   steering
e   tyres

## Question 3.59

Mark one answer

How can you reduce the chances of your car being broken into when leaving it unattended?

a   Take all contents with you
b   Park near a taxi rank
c   Place any valuables on the floor
d   Park near a fire station

## Question 3.60

Mark one answer

You have to leave valuables in your car. It would be safer to

a   put them in a carrier bag
b   park near a school entrance
c   lock them out of sight
d   park near a bus stop

## Question 3.61

Mark one answer

How could you deter theft from your car when leaving it unattended?

a   Leave valuables in a carrier bag
b   Lock valuables out of sight
c   Put valuables on the seats
d   Leave valuables on the floor

## Question 3.62

Mark one answer

Which of the following may help to deter a thief from stealing your car?

a   Always keeping the headlights on
b   Fitting reflective glass windows
c   Always keeping the interior light on
d   Etching the car number on the windows

## Question 3.63

Mark one answer

How can you help to prevent your car radio being stolen?

a Park in an unlit area
b Hide the radio with a blanket
c Park near a busy junction
d Install a security-coded radio

## Question 3.64

Mark one answer

Which of the following should not be kept in your vehicle?

a A first aid kit
b A road atlas
c The tax disc
d The vehicle documents

## Question 3.65

Mark one answer

What should you do when leaving your vehicle?

a Put valuable documents under the seats
b Remove all valuables
c Cover valuables with a blanket
d Leave the interior light on

## Question 3.66

Mark one answer

You are parking your car. You have some valuables which you are unable to take with you. What should you do?

a Park near a police station
b Put them under the driver's seat
c Lock them out of sight
d Park in an unlit side road

## Question 3.67

Mark one answer

Which of these is most likely to deter the theft of your vehicle?

a An immobiliser
b Tinted windows
c Locking wheel nuts
d A sun screen

## Question 3.68

Mark one answer

Wherever possible, which one of the following should you do when parking at night?

a Park in a quiet car park
b Park in a well lit area
c Park facing against the flow of traffic
d Park next to a busy junction

## Question 3.69

Mark one answer

When parking and leaving your car you should

a  park under a shady tree
b  remove the tax disc
c  park in a quiet road
d  engage the steering lock

## Question 3.70

Mark one answer

Rear facing baby seats should NEVER be used on a seat protected with

a  an airbag
b  seat belts
c  head restraints
d  seat covers

## Question 3.71

Mark one answer

When leaving your vehicle parked and unattended you should

a  park near a busy junction
b  park in a housing estate
c  remove the key and lock it
d  leave the left indicator on

## Question 3.72

Mark one answer

How can you lessen the risk of your vehicle being broken into at night?

a  Leave it in a well lit area
b  Park in a quiet side road
c  Don't engage the steering lock
d  Park in a poorly lit area

## Question 3.73

Mark one answer

To help keep your car secure you could join a

a  vehicle breakdown organisation
b  vehicle watch scheme
c  advanced drivers scheme
d  car maintenance class

## Question 3.74

Mark two answers

Which TWO of the following will improve fuel consumption?

a  Reducing your road speed
b  Planning well ahead
c  Late and harsh braking
d  Driving in lower gears
e  Short journeys with a cold engine
f  Rapid acceleration

## Question 3.75

Mark one answer

You service your own vehicle. How should you get rid of the old engine oil?

a   Take it to a local authority site
b   Pour it down a drain
c   Tip it into a hole in the ground
d   Put it into your dustbin

## Question 3.76

Mark one answer

On your vehicle, where would you find a catalytic converter?

a   In the fuel tank
b   In the air filter
c   On the cooling system
d   On the exhaust system

## Question 3.77

Mark one answer

Why do MOT tests include a strict exhaust emission test?

a   To recover the cost of expensive garage equipment
b   To help protect the environment against pollution
c   To discover which fuel supplier is used the most
d   To make sure diesel and petrol engines emit the same fumes

## Question 3.78

Mark three answers

To reduce the damage your vehicle causes to the environment you should

a   use narrow side streets
b   avoid harsh acceleration
c   brake in good time
d   anticipate well ahead
e   use busy routes

## Question 3.79

Mark one answer

Your vehicle has a catalytic converter. Its purpose is to reduce

a   exhaust noise
b   fuel consumption
c   exhaust emissions
d   engine noise

## Question 3.80

Mark two answers

A properly serviced vehicle will give

a   lower insurance premiums
b   you a refund on your road tax
c   better fuel economy
d   cleaner exhaust emissions

## Question 3.81

Mark one answer
You enter a road where there are road humps. What should you do?

a   Maintain a reduced speed throughout
b   Accelerate quickly between each one
c   Always keep to the maximum legal speed
d   Drive slowly at school times only

## Question 3.82

Mark one answer
When should you especially check the engine oil level?

a   Before a long journey
b   When the engine is hot
c   Early in the morning
d   Every 6000 miles

## Question 3.83

Mark one answer
You are having difficulty finding a parking space in a busy town. You can see there is space on the zigzag lines of a zebra crossing. Can you park there?

a   No, unless you stay with your car
b   Yes, in order to drop off a passenger
c   Yes, if you do not block people from crossing
d   No, not in any circumstances

## Question 3.84

Mark one answer
When leaving your car unattended for a few minutes you should

a   leave the engine running
b   switch the engine off but leave the key in
c   lock it and remove the key
d   park near a traffic warden

## Question 3.85

Mark one answer
When parking and leaving your car for a few minutes you should

a   leave it unlocked
b   lock it and remove the key
c   leave the hazard warning lights on
d   leave the interior light on

## Question 3.86

Mark one answer

When leaving your car, to help keep it secure you should

a    leave the hazard warning lights on
b    lock it and remove the key
c    park on a one way street
d    park in a residential area

## Question 3.87

Mark one answer

When leaving your vehicle where should you park if possible?

a    Opposite a traffic island
b    In a secure car park
c    On a bend
d    At or near a taxi rank

## Question 3.88

Mark one answer

You are leaving your vehicle parked on a road. When may you leave the engine running?

a    If you will be parking for less than five minutes
b    If the battery is flat
c    When in a 20mph zone
d    Never on any occasion

## Question 3.89

Mark three answers

In which THREE places would parking your vehicle cause danger or obstruction to other road users?

a    In front of a property entrance
b    At or near a bus stop
c    On your driveway
d    In a marked parking space
e    On the approach to a level crossing

## Question 3.90

Mark three answers
In which THREE places would parking cause an obstruction to others?

a    Near the brow of a hill
b    In a lay-by
c    Where the kerb is raised
d    Where the kerb has been lowered for wheelchairs
e    At or near a bus stop

## Question 3.91

Mark one answer
You are away from home and have to park your vehicle overnight. Where should you leave it?

a    Opposite another parked vehicle
b    In a quiet road
c    Opposite a traffic island
d    In a secure car park

## Answers and explanations

3.1     b A low level of brake fluid may cause your brakes to fail.

3.2     a, b

3.3     a, c, f

3.4     b, e, f

3.5     c The regulation only applies in a built up area.

3.6     a, b, f

3.7     c

3.8     b

3.9     a This is a traffic calming measure.

3.10     d

3.11     c

3.12     d

3.13     d

3.14     d

3.15     a

3.16     a, e

3.17     d Harsh braking is one of the major causes of high fuel consumption.

3.18     b

3.19     d The 'topping up' level will normally be marked on the battery.

3.20     d

3.21     a

3.22     b

3.23     b, c, d, f These must, by law, be in good working order.

3.24     d This helps the car operate more efficiently and cause less air pollution. Only unleaded fuel may be used.

3.25     d

3.26     b, c

3.27     b, c

3.28     a

3.29     d

3.30     c

3.31     a

3.32     b

3.33     b

3.34     d If you are involved in an accident, the head restraint helps protect your neck from whiplash.

3.35     c

3.36     d All passengers, front and rear, must wear seat belts, if fitted, unless exempt for medical reasons.

3.37     d

3.38     d Because it disturbs the airflow over your vehicle.

3.39     b

3.40     b

3.41     b

3.42     d

3.43     a, b

3.44     a, b, f

3.45     a, b, c

3.46     a, b, c

3.47     b, d, f

3.48     d

3.49     a, d, e

3.50     b, d, f A lot of short journeys use up a lot of petrol and pollute the atmosphere with the exhaust fumes.

3.51     d

3.52     b

3.53     c, d, e

| | | | |
|---|---|---|---|
| 3.54 | b | 3.75 | a |
| 3.55 | b | 3.76 | d |
| 3.56 | c | 3.77 | b |
| 3.57 | b | 3.78 | b, c, d |
| 3.58 | d, e | | |

3.59 a Your car is more likely to be broken into if valuables are visible through the windows.

3.78 b, c, d Doing these make for smoother driving which uses less fuel and so cuts down on pollution.

3.60 c

3.61 b

3.62 d Would-be thieves may well be able to steal any vehicle but if your vehicle is secured, and preferably alarmed or immobilised, they may leave it alone.

3.79 c

3.80 d

3.81 a Road humps are there to slow the traffic in residential areas.

3.82 a

3.63 d Having a security-coded radio makes your vehicle less desirable to a thief.

3.83 d

3.84 c

3.85 b

3.64 d

3.65 b

3.86 b

3.66 c

3.87 b

3.88 d

3.67 a An anti-theft device like an immobiliser makes it more difficult for the would-be thief to steal your car.

3.89 a, b, e

3.90 a, d, e

3.91 d

3.68 b

3.69 d

3.70 a The impact of the airbag, released in an accident, could kill a baby in a rear-facing baby seat.

3.71 c

3.72 a Avoid leaving your car unattended in poorly lit areas, especially if they are known to be high risk.

3.73 b

3.74 a, b

# Theory Test Questions for Car Drivers

2004–2005

Section 4     Safety margins

## Question 4.1

Braking distances on ice can be

a   twice the normal distance
b   five times the normal distance
c   seven times the normal distance
d   ten times the normal distance

## Question 4.2

Freezing conditions will affect the distance it takes you to come to a stop. You should expect stopping distances to increase by up to

a   two times
b   three times
c   five times
d   ten times

## Question 4.3

In very hot weather the road surface can get soft. Which TWO of the following will be affected most?

a   The suspension
b   The grip of the tyres
c   The braking
d   The exhaust

## Question 4.4

Where are you most likely to be affected by a sidewind?

a   On a narrow country lane
b   On an open stretch of road
c   On a busy stretch of road
d   On a long, straight road

## Question 4.5

In windy conditions you need to take extra care when

a   using the brakes
b   making a hill start
c   turning into a narrow road
d   passing pedal cyclists

## Question 4.6

What is the shortest stopping distance at 70mph?

a   53 metres (175 feet)
b   60 metres (197 feet)
c   73 metres (240 feet)
d   96 metres (315 feet)

## Question 4.7

Mark one answer

What is the shortest overall stopping distance on a dry road from 60 mph?

a 53 metres (175 feet)
b 58 metres (190 feet)
c 73 metres (240 feet)
d 96 metres (315 feet)

## Question 4.8

Mark one answer

Your indicators may be difficult to see in bright sunlight. What should you do?

a Put your indicator on earlier
b Give an arm signal as well as using your indicator
c Touch the brake several times to show the stop lights
d Turn as quickly as you can

## Question 4.9

Mark two answers

In very hot weather the road surface can get soft. Which TWO of the following will be affected most?

a The suspension
b The steering
c The braking
d The exhaust

## Question 4.10

Mark one answer

When approaching a right-hand bend you should keep well to the left. Why is this?

a To improve your view of the road
b To overcome the effect of the road's slope
c To let faster traffic from behind overtake
d To be positioned safely if you skid

## Question 4.11

Mark three answers

You should not overtake when

a intending to turn left shortly afterwards
b in a one-way street
c approaching a junction
d going up a long hill
e the view ahead is blocked

## Question 4.12

Mark one answer
You have just gone through deep water.
To dry off the brakes you should

a   accelerate and keep to a high speed
    for a short time
b   go slowly while gently applying the
    brakes
c   avoid using the brakes at all for
    a few miles
d   stop for at least an hour to allow
    them time to dry

## Question 4.13

Mark one answer
You are on a fast, open road in good
conditions. For safety, the distance
between you and the vehicle in front
should be

a   a two-second time gap
b   one car length
c   2 metres (6 feet 6 inches)
d   two car lengths

## Question 4.14

Mark one answer
What is the most common cause of
skidding?

a   Worn tyres
b   Driver error
c   Other vehicles
d   Pedestrians

## Question 4.15

Mark one answer
You are driving on an icy road. How can
you avoid wheelspin?

a   Drive at a slow speed in as high a
    gear as possible
b   Use the handbrake if the wheels start
    to slip
c   Brake gently and repeatedly
d   Drive in a low gear at all times

## Question 4.16

Mark one answer
Skidding is mainly caused by

a   the weather
b   the driver
c   the vehicle
d   the road

## Question 4.17

Mark two answers

You are driving in freezing conditions. What should you do when approaching a sharp bend?

a  Slow down before you reach the bend
b  Gently apply your handbrake
c  Firmly use your footbrake
d  Coast into the bend
e  Avoid sudden steering movements

## Question 4.18

Mark one answer

You are turning left on a slippery road. The back of your vehicle slides to the right. You should

a  brake firmly and not turn the steering wheel
b  steer carefully to the left
c  steer carefully to the right
d  brake firmly and steer to the left

## Question 4.19

Mark one answer

You are braking on a wet road. Your vehicle begins to skid. Your vehicle does not have anti-lock brakes. What is the FIRST thing you should do?

a  Quickly pull up the handbrake
b  Release the footbrake fully
c  Push harder on the brake pedal
d  Gently use the accelerator

## Question 4.20

Mark one answer
Coasting the vehicle

a  improves the driver's control
b  makes steering easier
c  reduces the driver's control
d  uses more fuel

## Question 4.21

Mark four answers

Before starting a journey in freezing weather you should clear ice and snow from your vehicle's

a  aerial
b  windows
c  bumper
d  lights
e  mirrors
f  number plates

## Question 4.22

Mark one answer

You are trying to move off on snow. You should use

a   the lowest gear you can
b   the highest gear you can
c   a high engine speed
d   the handbrake and footbrake together

## Question 4.23

Mark one answer

When driving in falling snow you should

a   brake firmly and quickly
b   be ready to steer sharply
c   use sidelights only
d   brake gently in plenty of time

## Question 4.24

Mark one answer

The MAIN benefit of having four-wheel drive is to improve

a   road holding
b   fuel consumption
c   stopping distances
d   passenger comfort

## Question 4.25

Mark one answer

You are about to go down a steep hill. To control the speed of your vehicle you should

a   select a high gear and use the brakes carefully
b   select a high gear and use the brakes firmly
c   select a low gear and use the brakes carefully
d   select a low gear and avoid using the brakes

## Question 4.26

Mark one answer

How can you use the engine of your vehicle as a brake?

a   By changing to a lower gear
b   By selecting reverse gear
c   By changing to a higher gear
d   By selecting neutral gear

## Question 4.27

Mark two answers

You wish to park facing DOWNHILL. Which TWO of the following should you do?

a   Turn the steering wheel towards the kerb
b   Park close to the bumper of another car
c   Park with two wheels on the kerb
d   Put the handbrake on firmly
e   Turn the steering wheel away from the kerb

## Question 4.28

Mark one answer

You are driving in a built-up area. You approach a speed hump. You should

a   move across to the left-hand side of the road
b   wait for any pedestrians to cross
c   slow your vehicle right down
d   stop and check both pavements

## Question 4.29

Mark one answer

You are on a long, downhill slope. What should you do to help control the speed of your vehicle?

a   Select neutral
b   Select a lower gear
c   Grip the handbrake firmly
d   Apply the parking brake gently

## Question 4.30 NI Exempt

Mark one answer

Your vehicle is fitted with anti-lock brakes. To stop quickly in an emergency you should

a   brake firmly and pump the brake pedal on and off
b   brake rapidly and firmly without releasing the brake pedal
c   brake gently and pump the brake pedal on and off
d   brake rapidly once, and immediately release the brake pedal

## Question 4.31

Mark one answer

Anti-lock brakes prevent wheels from locking. This means the tyres are less likely to

a   aquaplane
b   skid
c   puncture
d   wear

## Question 4.32

Mark one answer

Anti-lock brakes reduce the chances of a skid occurring particularly when

a   driving down steep hills
b   braking during normal driving
c   braking in an emergency
d   driving on good road surfaces

## Question 4.33 NI Exempt

Mark one answer

Anti-lock brakes are most effective when you

a   keep pumping the foot brake to prevent skidding
b   brake normally, but grip the steering wheel tightly
c   brake rapidly and firmly until you have slowed down
d   apply the handbrake to reduce the stopping distance

## Question 4.34 NI Exempt

Mark one answer

Your car is fitted with anti-lock brakes. You need to stop in an emergency. You should

a   brake normally and avoid turning the steering wheel
b   press the brake pedal rapidly and firmly until you have stopped
c   keep pushing and releasing the foot brake quickly to prevent skidding
d   apply the handbrake to reduce the stopping distance

## Question 4.35

Mark one answer

Vehicles fitted with anti-lock brakes

a   are impossible to skid
b   can be steered while you are braking
c   accelerate much faster
d   are not fitted with a handbrake

## Question 4.36

Mark two answers

Anti-lock brakes may not work as effectively if the road surface is

a   dry
b   loose
c   wet
d   good
e   firm

60

## Question 4.37

Mark one answer
Anti-lock brakes are of most use when you are

a   braking gently
b   driving on worn tyres
c   braking excessively
d   driving normally

## Question 4.38

Mark one answer
Driving a vehicle fitted with anti-lock brakes allows you to

a   brake harder because it is impossible to skid
b   drive at higher speeds
c   steer and brake at the same time
d   pay less attention to the road ahead

## Question 4.39

Mark one answer
Anti-lock brakes can greatly assist with

a   a higher cruising speed
b   steering control when braking
c   control when accelerating
d   motorway driving

## Question 4.40

Mark one answer
When would an anti-lock braking system start to work?

a   After the parking brake has been applied
b   Whenever pressure on the brake pedal is applied
c   Just as the wheels are about to lock
d   When the normal braking system fails to operate

## Question 4.41 NI Exempt

Mark one answer
You are driving a vehicle fitted with anti-lock brakes. You need to stop in an emergency. You should apply the footbrake

a   slowly and gently
b   slowly but firmly
c   rapidly and gently
d   rapidly and firmly

61

## Question 4.42

Mark two answers

Your vehicle has anti-lock brakes, but they may not always prevent skidding. This is most likely to happen when driving

a   in foggy conditions
b   on surface water
c   on loose road surfaces
d   on dry tarmac
e   at night on unlit roads

## Question 4.43

Mark one answer

Anti-lock brakes will take effect when

a   you do not brake quickly enough
b   excessive brake pressure has been applied
c   you have not seen a hazard ahead
d   speeding on slippery road surfaces

## Question 4.44

Mark three answers

When driving in fog, which of the following are correct?

a   Use dipped headlights
b   Use headlights on full beam
c   Allow more time for your journey
d   Keep close to the car in front
e   Slow down
f   Use side lights only

## Question 4.45

Mark one answer

You are driving along a country road. You see this sign. AFTER dealing safely with the hazard you should always

a   check your tyre pressures
b   switch on your hazard warning lights
c   accelerate briskly
d   test your brakes

## Question 4.46

Mark one answer

You are driving in heavy rain. Your steering suddenly becomes very light. You should

a   steer towards the side of the road
b   apply gentle acceleration
c   brake firmly to reduce speed
d   ease off the accelerator

## Question 4.47

Mark one answer

How can you tell when you are driving over black ice?

a   It is easier to brake
b   The noise from your tyres sounds louder
c   You see black ice on the road
d   Your steering feels light

## Question 4.48

Mark one answer

The roads are icy. You should drive slowly

a   in the highest gear possible
b   in the lowest gear possible
c   with the handbrake partly on
d   with your left foot on the brake

## Question 4.49

Mark one answer

You are driving along a wet road. How can you tell if your vehicle is aquaplaning?

a   The engine will stall
b   The engine noise will increase
c   The steering will feel very heavy
d   The steering will feel very light

## Question 4.50

Mark two answers

How can you tell if you are driving on ice?

a   The tyres make a rumbling noise
b   The tyres make hardly any noise
c   The steering becomes heavier
d   The steering becomes lighter

## Question 4.51

Mark one answer

You are driving along a wet road. How can you tell if your vehicle's tyres are losing their grip on the surface?

a   The engine will stall
b   The steering will feel very heavy
c   The engine noise will increase
d   The steering will feel very light

## Question 4.52

Mark one answer

You are travelling at 50mph on a good, dry road. What is your shortest overall stopping distance?

a   36 metres (120 feet)
b   53 metres (175 feet)
c   75 metres (245 feet)
d   96 metres (315 feet)

## Question 4.53

Mark one answer
Your overall stopping distance will be much longer when driving

a   in the rain
b   in fog
c   at night
d   in strong winds

## Question 4.54

Mark one answer
You have driven through a flood. What is the first thing you should do?

a   Stop and check the tyres
b   Stop and dry the brakes
c   Check your exhaust
d   Test your brakes

## Question 4.55

Mark one answer
You are on a good, dry road surface. Your vehicle has good brakes and tyres. What is the BRAKING distance at 50mph?

a   38 metres (125 feet)
b   14 metres (46 feet)
c   24 metres (79 feet)
d   55 metres (180 feet)

## Question 4.56

Mark one answer
You are on a good, dry road surface and your vehicle has good brakes and tyres. What is the typical overall stopping distance at 40mph?

a   23 metres (75 feet)
b   36 metres (120 feet)
c   53 metres (175 feet)
d   96 metres (315 feet)

## Answers and explanations

4.1  d

4.2  d

4.3  b, c

4.4  b

4.5  d In windy conditions cyclists are all too easily blown about and may wobble or steer off course.

4.6  d

4.7  c

4.8  b

4.9  b, c

4.10 a You can see further round the bend earlier if you keep to the left.

4.11 a, c, e

4.12 b

4.13 a

4.14 b

4.15 a

4.16 b Skidding is usually caused by harsh braking, harsh acceleration or harsh steering – all actions of the driver. You are, however, more likely to cause a skid in a poorly maintained car, in bad weather or on a poor road surface.

4.17 a, e

Braking on an icy bend is extremely dangerous. It could cause your vehicle to spin.

4.18 c

4.19 b Note that the question asks for the first thing you should do, which is always to remove the cause of the skid – in this case braking. You would next need to re-apply the brakes more gently. 'c' is wrong because braking harder would increase the skid.

4.20 c Coasting means driving along with the clutch pedal down. This disconnects the engine and gears from the drive wheels of the car, so you have less control.

4.21 b, d, e, f

4.22 b

4.23 d

4.24 a

4.25 c A low gear will help control your speed, but on a steep hill you will also need your brakes.

4.26 a

4.27 a, d

If the handbrake should fail, the car will roll into the kerb and not down the road.

4.28 c

4.29 b You should ideally have selected the lower gear before starting down the slope. 'a' would be likely to make your car go faster as you would no longer be in any gear at all.

4.30 b

4.31 b

4.32 c You should brake rapidly and firmly.

4.33 c

4.34 b

4.35   b A vehicle fitted with anti-lock brakes is very difficult, but not impossible, to skid. Take care if the road surface is loose or wet.

4.36   b, c

4.37   c

4.38   c

4.39   b

4.40   c

4.41   d

4.42   b, c

4.43   b

4.44   a, c, e

4.45   d Drive slowly forwards with your left foot gently on the footbrake. This helps dry out the brakes.

4.46   d

4.47   d Black ice is normally invisible when you are driving. The tyres will lose grip with the road which will make the steering feel light.

4.48   a

4.49   d

4.50   b, d

4.51   d This problem is sometimes called aquaplaning. Your tyres build up a thin film of water between them and the road and lose all grip. The steering suddenly feels light and probably uncontrollable. The solution is to ease off the accelerator until you feel the tyres grip the road again.

4.52   b

4.53   a

4.54   d Your brakes may be wet. The first thing you should do is check them and then dry them.

4.55   a Note this is the braking distance. The overall stopping distance is further because you have to add 'thinking' distance.

4.56   b

# Theory Test Questions for Car Drivers

2004–2005

Section 5    Hazard perception

## Question 5.1

Mark one answer
You see this sign on the rear of a slow-moving lorry that you want to pass. It is travelling in the middle lane of a three-lane motorway. You should

a   cautiously approach the lorry then pass on either side
b   follow the lorry until you can leave the motorway
c   wait on the hard shoulder until the lorry has stopped
d   approach with care and keep to the left of the lorry

## Question 5.2

Mark two answers
Where would you expect to see these markers?

a   On a motorway sign
b   At the entrance to a narrow bridge
c   On a large goods vehicle
d   On a builder's skip placed on the road

## Question 5.3

Mark one answer
What does this signal from a police officer mean to oncoming traffic?

a   Go ahead
b   Stop
c   Turn left
d   Turn right

## Question 5.4

Mark one answer
What is the main hazard shown in this picture?

a   Vehicles turning right
b   Vehicles doing U-turns
c   The cyclist crossing the road
d   Parked cars around the corner

## Question 5.5

Mark one answer

Which road user has caused a hazard?

a The parked car (arrowed A)
b The pedestrian waiting to cross (arrowed B)
c The moving car (arrowed C)
d The car turning (arrowed D)

## Question 5.6

Mark one answer

What should the driver of the car approaching the crossing do?

a Continue at the same speed
b Sound the horn
c Drive through quickly
d Slow down and get ready to stop

## Question 5.7

Mark three answers

What THREE things should the driver of the grey car (arrowed) be especially aware of?

a Pedestrians stepping out between cars
b Other cars behind the grey car
c Doors opening on parked cars
d The bumpy road surface
e Cars leaving parking spaces
f Empty parking spaces

## Question 5.8

Mark one answer

You think the driver of the vehicle in front has forgotten to cancel the right indicator. You should

a flash your lights to alert the driver
b sound your horn before overtaking
c overtake on the left if there is room
d stay behind and not overtake

## Question 5.9

Mark one answer
In heavy motorway traffic you are being followed closely by the vehicle behind. How can you lower the risk of an accident?

a   Increase your distance from the vehicle in front

b   Tap your foot on the brake pedal sharply

c   Switch on your hazard lights

d   Move onto the hard shoulder and stop

## Question 5.10

Mark one answer
What is the main hazard the driver of the red car (arrowed) should be most aware

a   Glare from the sun may affect the driver's vision

b   The black car may stop suddenly

c   The bus may move out into the road

d   Oncoming vehicles will assume the driver is turning right

## Question 5.11

Mark one answer
You see this sign ahead. You should expect the road to

a   go steeply uphill

b   go steeply downhill

c   bend sharply to the left

d   bend sharply to the right

## Question 5.12

Mark one answer

You are approaching this cyclist.
You should

a  overtake before the cyclist gets to
   the junction
b  flash your headlights at the cyclist
c  slow down and allow the cyclist to turn
d  overtake the cyclist on the left-hand
   side

## Question 5.13

Mark one answer

Why must you take extra care when
turning right at this junction?

a  Road surface is poor
b  Footpaths are narrow
c  Road markings are faint
d  There is reduced visibility

## Question 5.14

Mark one answer

This yellow sign on a vehicle indicates
this is

a  a vehicle broken down
b  a school bus
c  an ice cream van
d  a private ambulance

## Question 5.15

Mark one answer

When approaching this bridge you
should give way to

a  bicycles
b  buses
c  motorcycles
d  cars

## Question 5.16

Mark one answer
What type of vehicle could you expect to meet in the middle of the road?

a Lorry
b Bicycle
c Car
d Motorcycle

## Question 5.17

Mark one answer
At this blind junction you must stop

a behind the line, then edge forward to see clearly
b beyond the line at a point where you can see clearly
c only if there is traffic on the main road
d only if you are turning to the right

## Question 5.18

Mark one answer
A driver pulls out of a side road in front of you. You have to brake hard. You should

a ignore the error and stay calm
b flash your lights to show your annoyance
c sound your horn to show your annoyance
d overtake as soon as possible

## Question 5.19

Mark one answer
An elderly person's driving ability could be affected because they may be unable to

a obtain car insurance
b understand road signs
c react very quickly
d give signals correctly

## Question 5.20

Mark one answer
You have just passed these warning lights. What hazard would you expect to see next?

a A level crossing with no barrier
b An ambulance station
c A school crossing patrol
d An opening bridge

## Question 5.21

Mark two answers
Why should you be especially cautious when going past this bus?

a  There is traffic approaching in the distance

b  The driver may open the door

c  It may suddenly move off

d  People may cross the road in front of it

e  There are bicycles parked on the pavement

## Question 5.22

Mark one answer
In areas where there are 'traffic calming' measures you should

a  drive at a reduced speed

b  always drive at the speed limit

c  position in the centre of the road

d  only slow down if pedestrians are near

## Question 5.23

Mark one answer
You are planning a long journey. Do you need to plan rest stops?

a  Yes, you should plan to stop every half an hour

b  Yes, regular stops help concentration

c  No, you will be less tired if you get there as soon as possible

d  No, only fuel stops will be needed

## Question 5.24

Mark one answer
The red lights are flashing. What should you do when approaching this level crossing?

a  Go through quickly

b  Go through carefully

c  Stop before the barrier

d  Switch on hazard warning lights

## Question 5.25

Mark one answer
A driver does something that upsets you. You should

a   try not to react
b   let them know how you feel
c   flash your headlights several times
d   sound your horn

## Question 5.26

Mark two answers
What are TWO main hazards you should be aware of when going along this street?

a   Glare from the sun
b   Car doors opening suddenly
c   Lack of road markings
d   The headlights on parked cars being switched on
e   Large goods vehicles
f   Children running out from between vehicles

## Question 5.27

Mark one answer
What is the main hazard you should be aware of when following this cyclist?

a   The cyclist may move into the left and dismount
b   The cyclist may swerve out into the road
c   The contents of the cyclist's carrier may fall onto the road
d   The cyclist may wish to turn right at the end of the road

## Question 5.28

Mark one answer
A driver's behaviour has upset you. It may help if you

a   stop and take a break
b   shout abusive language
c   gesture to them with your hand
d   follow their car, flashing the headlights

## Question 5.29

Mark two answers

When approaching this hazard why should you slow down?

a   Because of the bend
b   Because it's hard to see to the right
c   Because of approaching traffic
d   Because of animals crossing
e   Because of the level crossing

## Question 5.30

Mark one answer

You are on a dual carriageway. Ahead you see a vehicle with an amber flashing light. What will this be?

a   An ambulance
b   A fire engine
c   A doctor on call
d   A disabled persons vehicle

## Question 5.31

Mark one answer

You are approaching crossroads. The traffic lights have failed. What should you do?

a   Brake and stop only for large vehicles
b   Brake sharply to a stop before looking
c   Be prepared to brake sharply to a stop
d   Be prepared to stop for any traffic

## Question 5.32

Mark one answer

What should the driver of the red car (arrowed) do?

a   Wave the pedestrians who are waiting to cross
b   Wait for the pedestrian in the road to cross
c   Quickly drive behind the pedestrian in the road
d   Tell the pedestrian in the road she should not have crossed

## Question 5.33

Mark one answer
Why are destination markings painted on the road surface?

a   To restrict the flow of traffic
b   To warn you of oncoming traffic
c   To enable you to change lanes early
d   To prevent you changing lanes

## Question 5.34

Mark one answer
You are following a slower-moving vehicle on a narrow country road. There is a junction just ahead on the right. What should you do?

a   Overtake after checking your mirrors and signalling
b   Stay behind until you are past the junction
c   Accelerate quickly to pass before the junction
d   Slow down and prepare to overtake on the left

## Question 5.35

Mark one answer
What should you do as you approach this overhead bridge?

a   Move out to the centre of the road before going through
b   Find another route, this is only for high vehicles
c   Be prepared to give way to large vehicles in the middle of the road
d   Move across to the right-hand side before going through

## Question 5.36

Mark one answer
Why are mirrors often slightly curved (convex)?

a   They give a wider field of vision
b   They totally cover blind spots
c   They make it easier to judge the speed of following traffic
d   They make following traffic look bigger

## Question 5.37

Mark one answer

What does the solid white line at the side of the road indicate?

a Traffic lights ahead
b Edge of the carriageway
c Footpath on the left
d Cycle path

## Question 5.38

Mark one answer

You are driving towards this level crossing. What would be the first warning of an approaching train?

a Both half barriers down
b A steady amber light
c One half barrier down
d Twin flashing red lights

## Question 5.39

Mark two answers

You are driving along this motorway. It is raining. When following this lorry you should

a allow at least a two-second gap
b move left and drive on the hard shoulder
c allow at least a four-second gap
d be aware of spray reducing your vision
e move right and stay in the right-hand lane

## Question 5.40

Mark one answer

You are behind this cyclist. When the traffic lights change, what should you do?

a  Try to move off before the cyclist
b  Allow the cyclist time and room
c  Turn right but give the cyclist room
d  Tap your horn and drive through first

## Question 5.41

Mark one answer
You are driving towards this left-hand bend. What dangers should you be aware of?

a  A vehicle overtaking you
b  No white lines in the centre of the road
c  No sign to warn you of the bend
d  Pedestrians walking towards you

## Question 5.42

Mark one answer
While driving, you see this sign ahead. You should

a  stop at the sign
b  slow, but continue around the bend
c  slow to a crawl and continue
d  stop and look for open farm gates

## Question 5.43

Mark one answer
Why should the junction on the left be kept clear?

a  To allow vehicles to enter and emerge
b  To allow the bus to reverse
c  To allow vehicles to make a 'U' turn
d  To allow vehicles to park

## Question 5.44

Mark one answer
When the traffic lights change to green the white car should

a   wait for the cyclist to pull away
b   move off quickly and turn in front of the cyclist
c   move close up to the cyclist to beat the lights
d   sound the horn to warn the cyclist

## Question 5.45

Mark one answer
You intend to turn left at the traffic lights. Just before turning you should

a   check your right mirror
b   move close up to the white car
c   straddle the lanes
d   check for bicycles on your left

## Question 5.46

Mark one answer
You should reduce your speed when driving along this road because

a   there is a staggered junction ahead
b   there is a low bridge ahead
c   there is a change in the road surface
d   the road ahead narrows

## Question 5.47

Mark one answer
You are driving at 60mph. As you approach this hazard you should

a   maintain your speed
b   reduce your speed
c   take the next right turn
d   take the next left turn

## Question 5.48

Mark two answers

The traffic ahead of you in the left lane is slowing. You should

a  be wary of cars on your right cutting in

b  accelerate past the vehicles in the left lane

c  pull up on the left-hand verge

d  move across and continue in the right-hand lane

e  slow down, keeping a safe separation distance

## Question 5.49

Mark one answer

What might you expect to happen in this situation?

a  Traffic will move into the right-hand lane

b  Traffic speed will increase

c  Traffic will move into the left-hand lane

d  Traffic will not need to change position

## Question 5.50

Mark one answer

You are driving on a road with several lanes. You see these signs above the lanes. What do they mean?

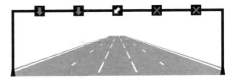

a  The two right lanes are open

b  The two left lanes are open

c  Traffic in the left lanes should stop

d  Traffic in the right lanes should stop

## Question 5.51

Mark two answers

As a provisional licence holder, you must not drive a motor car

a  at more than 50mph

b  on your own

c  on the motorway

d  under the age of 18 years of age at night

e  with passengers in the rear seats

## Question 5.52

Mark one answer
After passing your driving test, you suffer from ill health. This affects your driving. You MUST

a   inform your local police station
b   get on as best you can
c   not inform anyone as you hold a full licence
d   inform the licensing authority

## Question 5.53

Mark one answer
You are invited to a pub lunch. You know that you will have to drive in the evening. What is your best course of action?

a   Avoid mixing your alcoholic drinks
b   Not drink any alcohol at all
c   Have some milk before drinking alcohol
d   Eat a hot meal with your alcoholic drinks

## Question 5.54

Mark one answer
You have been convicted of driving while unfit through drink or drugs. You will find this is likely to cause the cost of one of the following to rise considerably. Which one?

a   Road fund licence
b   Insurance premiums
c   Vehicle test certificate
d   Driving licence

## Question 5.55

Mark one answer
What advice should you give to a driver who has had a few alcoholic drinks at a party?

a   Have a strong cup of coffee and then drive home
b   Drive home carefully and slowly
c   Go home by public transport
d   Wait a short while and then drive home

## Question 5.56

Mark one answer

You have been taking medicine for a few days which made you feel drowsy. Today you feel better but still need to take the medicine. You should only drive

a   if your journey is necessary
b   at night on quiet roads
c   if someone goes with you
d   after checking with your doctor

## Question 5.57

Mark one answer

You are about to return home from holiday when you become ill. A doctor prescribes drugs which are likely to affect your driving. You should

a   drive only if someone is with you
b   avoid driving on motorways
c   not drive yourself
d   never drive at more than 30mph

## Question 5.58

Mark two answers

During periods of illness your ability to drive may be impaired. You MUST

a   see your doctor each time before you drive
b   only take smaller doses of any medicines
c   be medically fit to drive
d   not drive after taking certain medicines
e   take all your medicines with you when you drive

## Question 5.59

Mark two answers

You feel drowsy when driving. You should

a   stop and rest as soon as possible
b   turn the heater up to keep you warm and comfortable
c   make sure you have a good supply of fresh air
d   continue with your journey but drive more slowly
e   close the car windows to help you concentrate

## Question 5.60

Mark two answers

You are driving along a motorway and become tired. You should

a   stop at the next service area and rest
b   leave the motorway at the next exit and rest
c   increase your speed and turn up the radio volume
d   close all your windows and set heating to warm
e   pull up on the hard shoulder and change drivers

## Question 5.61

Mark one answer

You are taking drugs that are likely to affect your driving. What should you do?

a   Seek medical advice before driving
b   Limit your driving to essential journeys
c   Only drive if accompanied by a full licence-holder
d   Drive only for short distances

## Question 5.62

Mark one answer

You are about to drive home. You feel very tired and have a severe headache. You should

a   wait until you are fit and well before driving
b   drive home, but take a tablet for headaches
c   drive home if you can stay awake for the journey
d   wait for a short time, then drive home slowly

## Question 5.63

Mark one answer

If you are feeling tired it is best to stop as soon as you can. Until then you should

a   increase your speed to find a stopping place quickly
b   ensure a supply of fresh air
c   gently tap the steering wheel
d   keep changing speed to improve concentration

## Question 5.64

Mark one answer

If your motorway journey seems boring and you feel drowsy whilst driving you should

a  open a window and drive to the next service area
b  stop on the hard shoulder for a sleep
c  speed up to arrive at your destination sooner
d  slow down and let other drivers overtake

## Question 5.65

Mark three answers

Driving long distances can be tiring. You can prevent this by

a  stopping every so often for a walk
b  opening a window for some fresh air
c  ensuring plenty of refreshment breaks
d  completing the journey without stopping
e  eating a large meal before driving

## Question 5.66

Mark one answer

You go to a social event and need to drive a short time after. What precaution should you take?

a  Avoid drinking alcohol on an empty stomach
b  Drink plenty of coffee after drinking alcohol
c  Avoid drinking alcohol completely
d  Drink plenty of milk before drinking alcohol

## Question 5.67

Mark one answer

You take some cough medicine given to you by a friend. What should you do before driving?

a  Ask your friend if taking the medicine affected their driving
b  Drink some strong coffee one hour before driving
c  Check the label to see if the medicine will affect your driving
d  Drive a short distance to see if the medicine is affecting your driving

## Question 5.68

Mark one answer

You take the wrong route and find you
are on a one-way street. You should

a   reverse out of the road
b   turn round in a side road
c   continue to the end of the road
d   reverse into a driveway

## Question 5.69

Mark three answers

Which THREE are likely to make you lose
concentration while driving?

a   Looking at road maps
b   Listening to loud music
c   Using your windscreen washers
d   Looking in your wing mirror
e   Using a mobile phone

## Question 5.70

Mark one answer

You are driving along this road. The driver
on the left is reversing from a driveway.
You should

a   move to the opposite side of the road
b   drive through as you have priority
c   sound your horn and be prepared
    to stop
d   speed up and drive through quickly

## Question 5.71

Mark one answer

You have been involved in an argument
before starting your journey. This has
made you feel angry. You should

a   start to drive, but open a window
b   drive slower than normal and turn
    your radio on
c   have an alcoholic drink to help you
    relax before driving
d   calm down before you start to drive

## Question 5.72

Mark one answer

You start to feel tired while driving.
What should you do?

a  Increase your speed slightly
b  Decrease your speed slightly
c  Find a less busy route
d  Pull over at a safe place to rest

## Question 5.73

Mark one answer
You are driving on this dual carriageway.
Why may you need to slow down?

a  There is a broken white line in the centre
b  There are solid white lines either side
c  There are roadworks ahead of you
d  There are no footpaths

## Question 5.74

Mark one answer
You have just been overtaken by this
motorcyclist who is cutting in sharply.
You should

a  sound the horn
b  brake firmly
c  keep a safe gap
d  flash your lights

## Question 5.75

Mark one answer
You are about to drive home. You cannot
find the glasses you need to wear. You
should

a  drive home slowly, keeping to quiet roads
b  borrow a friend's glasses and use those
c  drive home at night, so that the lights will help you
d  find a way of getting home without driving

## Question 5.76

Mark three answers

Which THREE result from drinking alcohol?

a Less control
b A false sense of confidence
c Faster reactions
d Poor judgement of speed
e Greater awareness of danger

## Question 5.77

Mark three answers

Which THREE of these are likely effects of drinking alcohol?

a Reduced co-ordination
b Increased confidence
c Poor judgement
d Increased concentration
e Faster reactions
f Colour blindness

## Question 5.78

Mark one answer

How does alcohol affect you?

a It speeds up your reactions
b It increases your awareness
c It improves your co-ordination
d It reduces your concentration

## Question 5.79

Mark one answer

Your doctor has given you a course of medicine. Why should you ask how it will affect you?

a Drugs make you a better driver by quickening your reactions
b You will have to let your insurance company know about the medicine
c Some types of medicine can cause your reactions to slow down
d The medicine you take may affect your hearing

## Question 5.80

Mark two answers

You are not sure if your cough medicine will affect you. What TWO things could you do?

a Ask your doctor
b Check the medicine label
c Drive if you feel alright
d Ask a friend or relative for advice

## Question 5.81

Mark one answer
You are on a motorway. You feel tired. You should

a carry on but go slowly
b leave the motorway at the next exit
c complete your journey as quickly as possible
d stop on the hard shoulder

## Question 5.82

Mark one answer
You find that you need glasses to read vehicle number plates at the required distance. When MUST you wear them?

a Only in bad weather conditions
b At all times when driving
c Only when you think it necessary
d Only in bad light or at night time

## Question 5.83

Mark two answers
Which TWO things would help to keep you alert during a long journey?

a Finishing your journey as fast as you can
b Keeping off the motorways and using country roads
c Making sure that you get plenty of fresh air
d Making regular stops for refreshments

## Question 5.84

Mark one answer
Which of the following types of glasses should NOT be worn when driving at night?

a Half-moon
b Round
c Bi-focal
d Tinted

## Question 5.85

Mark three answers
Drinking any amount of alcohol is likely to

a slow down your reactions to hazards
b increase the speed of your reactions
c worsen your judgement of speed
d improve your awareness of danger
e give a false sense of confidence

## Question 5.86

Mark three answers
What else can seriously affect your concentration, other than alcoholic drinks?

a Drugs
b Tiredness
c Tinted windows
d Contact lenses
e Loud music

88

## Question 5.87

Mark one answer
As a driver you find that your eyesight has become very poor. Your optician says they cannot help you. The law says that you should tell

a the licensing authority
b your own doctor
c the local police station
d another optician

## Question 5.88

Mark one answer
For which of these may you use hazard warning lights?

a When driving on a motorway to warn traffic behind of a hazard ahead
b When you are double-parked on a two-way road
c When your direction indicators are not working
d When warning oncoming traffic that you intend to stop

## Question 5.89

Mark one answer
When should you use hazard warning lights?

a When you are double-parked on a two-way road
b When your direction indicators are not working
c When warning oncoming traffic that you intend to stop
d When your vehicle has broken down and is causing an obstruction

## Question 5.90

Mark one answer
You want to turn left at this junction. The view of the main road is restricted. What should you do?

a Stay well back and wait to see if something comes
b Build up your speed so that you can emerge quickly
c Stop and apply the handbrake even if the road is clear
d Approach slowly and edge out until you can see more clearly

## Question 5.91

Mark one answer

You are driving on a motorway. The traffic ahead is braking sharply because of an accident. How could you warn following traffic?

a   Briefly use the hazard warning lights
b   Switch on the hazard warning lights continuously
c   Briefly use the rear fog lights
d   Switch on the headlamps continuously

## Question 5.92

Mark one answer

When may you use hazard warning lights?

a   To park alongside another car
b   To park on double yellow lines
c   When you are being towed
d   When you have broken down

## Question 5.93

Mark one answer

Hazard warning lights should be used when vehicles are

a   broken down and causing an obstruction
b   faulty and moving slowly
c   being towed along a road
d   reversing into a side road

## Question 5.94

Mark one answer

When driving a car fitted with automatic transmission what would you use 'kick down' for?

a   Cruise control
b   Quick acceleration
c   Slow braking
d   Fuel economy

## Answers and explanations

5.1   d
5.2   c, d
5.3   b
5.4   c
5.5   a
5.6   d
5.7   a, c, e
5.8   d
5.9   a
5.10  c
5.11  c
5.12  c
5.13  d
5.14  b
5.15  b
5.16  a
5.17  a
5.18  a
5.19  c
5.20  c
5.21  c, d
5.22  a Road humps and rumble strips are examples of traffic calming measures. They are often found in residential areas and have been introduced to reduce the overall speed of traffic.
5.23  b
5.24  c
5.25  a
5.26  b, f
5.27  b
5.28  a
5.29  a, e
5.30  d
5.31  d
5.32  b

5.33  c
5.34  b
5.35  c
5.36  a
5.37  b
5.38  b
5.39  c, d
5.40  b
5.41  d
5.42  b
5.43  a
5.44  a
5.45  d
5.46  a
5.47  b
5.48  a, e
5.49  c
5.50  b
5.51  b, c
5.52  d In the event of a short-term illness, like flu, that affected your ability to drive, you would simply not drive until you are recovered.
5.53  b
5.54  b
5.55  c The only sensible answer is don't drink and drive.
5.56  d
5.57  c
5.58  c, d
5.59  a, c
5.60  a, b
5.61  a A significant number of drugs, even those you can buy in the chemist, can affect your ability to drive. Sometimes a warning is given on the packet, but if in any doubt seek medical advice.

5.62   a
5.63   b
5.64   a
5.65   a, b, c
5.66   c
5.67   c
5.68   c
5.69   a, b, e
        'c' and 'd' are normal parts of the driving task.
5.70   c
5.71   d
5.72   d
5.73   c
5.74   c
5.75   d
5.76   a, b, d
5.77   a, b, c
5.78   d You may well feel, after drinking, that 'a', 'b' and 'c' are true. However, this is never correct and makes you dangerous.
5.79   c
5.80   a, b
5.81   b If you feel tired you greatly increase your chances of having an accident. You must stop, but as you are on a motorway you cannot do this unless you leave at the next exit or find a service station before it.
5.82   b If you need glasses to drive you must wear them whenever you are driving, so 'b' is correct.
5.83   c, d
5.84   d
5.85   a, c, e
5.86   a, b, e

5.87   a You must not drive if your eyesight becomes so poor that you can no longer meet the minimum legal requirements, wearing glasses or contact lenses if necessary.
5.88   a
5.89   d
5.90   d
5.91   a
5.92   d
5.93   a
5.94   b

# Theory Test Questions for Car Drivers

2004–2005

Section 6    Vulnerable road users

## Question 6.1

Mark one answer
Which sign means that there may be people walking along the road?

a

b

c

d

## Question 6.2

Mark one answer
You are turning left at a junction. Pedestrians have started to cross the road. You should

a go on, giving them plenty of room
b stop and wave at them to cross
c blow your horn and proceed
d give way to them

## Question 6.3

Mark one answer
You are turning left from a main road into a side road. People are already crossing the road into which you are turning. You should

a continue, as it is your right of way
b signal to them to continue crossing
c wait and allow them to cross
d sound your horn to warn them of your presence

## Question 6.4

Mark one answer
You are at a road junction, turning into a minor road. There are pedestrians crossing the minor road. You should

a stop and wave the pedestrians across
b sound your horn to let the pedestrians know that you are there
c give way to the pedestrians who are already crossing
d carry on; the pedestrians should give way to you

## Question 6.5

Mark one answer
You are turning left into a side road.
What hazards should you be especially
aware of?

a  One-way street
b  Pedestrians
c  Traffic congestion
d  Parked vehicles

## Question 6.6

Mark one answer
You intend to turn right into a side road.
Just before turning you should check for
motorcyclists who might be

a  overtaking on your left
b  following you closely
c  emerging from the side road
d  overtaking on your right

## Question 6.7

Mark one answer
A toucan crossing is different from other
crossings because

a  moped riders can use it
b  it is controlled by a traffic warden
c  it is controlled by two flashing lights
d  cyclists can use it

## Question 6.8

Mark two answers
At toucan crossings

a  there is no flashing amber light
b  cyclists are not permitted
c  there is a continuously flashing amber
   beacon
d  pedestrians and cyclists may cross
e  you only stop if someone is waiting to
   cross

## Question 6.9

Mark one answer
What does this sign tell you?

a  No cycling
b  Cycle route ahead
c  Route for cycles only
d  End of cycle route

## Question 6.10

Mark one answer
How will a school-crossing patrol signal
you to stop?

a  By pointing to children on the
   opposite pavement
b  By displaying a red light
c  By displaying a stop sign
d  By giving you an arm signal

## Question 6.11

Mark one answer
Where would you see this sign?

a   In the window of a car taking children to school
b   At the side of the road
c   At playground areas
d   On the rear of a school bus or coach

## Question 6.12

Mark one answer
Which sign tells you that pedestrians may be walking in the road as there is no pavement?

a   b

c   d

## Question 6.13

Mark one answer
What does this sign mean?

a   No route for pedestrians and cyclists
b   A route for pedestrians only
c   A route for cyclists only
d   A route for pedestrians and cyclists

## Question 6.14

Mark one answer
You see a pedestrian with a white stick and red band. This means that the person is

a   physically disabled
b   deaf only
c   blind only
d   deaf and blind

## Question 6.15

Mark one answer
What action would you take when elderly people are crossing the road?

a Wave them across so they know that you have seen them

b Be patient and allow them to cross in their own time

c Rev the engine to let them know that you are waiting

d Tap the horn in case they are hard of hearing

## Question 6.16

Mark one answer
You see two elderly pedestrians about to cross the road ahead. You should

a expect them to wait for you to pass

b speed up to get past them quickly

c stop and wave them across the road

d be careful, they may misjudge your speed

## Question 6.17

Mark one answer
What does this sign mean?

a Contraflow pedal cycle lane

b With-flow pedal cycle lane

c Pedal cycles and buses only

d No pedal cycles or buses

## Question 6.18

Mark one answer
You are coming up to a roundabout. A cyclist is signalling to turn right. What should you do?

a Overtake on the right

b Give a horn warning

c Signal the cyclist to move across

d Give the cyclist plenty of room

## Question 6.19

Mark one answer
You are approaching this roundabout and see the cyclist signal right. Why is the cyclist keeping to the left?

a   It is a quicker route for the cyclist
b   The cyclist is going to turn left instead
c   The cyclist thinks The Highway Code does not apply to bicycles
d   The cyclist is slower and more vulnerable

## Question 6.20

Mark one answer
When you are overtaking a cyclist you should leave as much room as you would give to a car. What is the main reason for this?

a   The cyclist might change lanes
b   The cyclist might get off the bike
c   The cyclist might swerve
d   The cyclist might have to make a right turn

## Question 6.21

Mark two answers
Which TWO should you allow extra room when overtaking?

a   Motorcycles
b   Tractors
c   Bicycles
d   Road-sweeping vehicles

## Question 6.22

Mark one answer
Why should you look particularly for motorcyclists and cyclists at junctions?

a   They may want to turn into the side road
b   They may slow down to let you turn
c   They are harder to see
d   They might not see you turn

## Question 6.23

Mark one answer
You are waiting to come out of a side road. Why should you watch carefully for motorcycles?

a   Motorcycles are usually faster than cars
b   Police patrols often use motorcycles
c   Motorcycles are small and hard to see
d   Motorcycles have right of way

## Question 6.24

Mark one answer
In daylight, an approaching motorcyclist is using a dipped headlight. Why?

a  So that the rider can be seen more easily
b  To stop the battery overcharging
c  To improve the rider's vision
d  The rider is inviting you to proceed

## Question 6.25

Mark one answer
Motorcyclists should wear bright clothing mainly because

a  they must do so by law
b  it helps keep them cool in summer
c  the colours are popular
d  drivers often do not see them

## Question 6.26

Mark one answer
There is a slow-moving motorcyclist ahead of you. You are unsure what the rider is going to do. You should

a  pass on the left
b  pass on the right
c  stay behind
d  move closer

## Question 6.27

Mark one answer
Motorcyclists will often look round over their right shoulder just before turning right. This is because

a  they need to listen for following traffic
b  motorcycles do not have mirrors
c  looking around helps them balance as they turn
d  they need to check for traffic in their blind area

## Question 6.28

Mark three answers
At road junctions which of the following are most vulnerable?

a  Cyclists
b  Motorcyclists
c  Pedestrians
d  Car drivers
e  Lorry drivers

## Question 6.29

Mark one answer
Motorcyclists are particularly vulnerable

a  when moving off
b  on dual carriageways
c  when approaching junctions
d  on motorways

## Question 6.30

Mark one answer
An injured motorcyclist is lying unconscious in the road. You should

a   remove the safety helmet
b   seek medical assistance
c   move the person off the road
d   remove the leather jacket

## Question 6.31

Mark one answer
You notice horse riders in front. What should you do FIRST?

a   Pull out to the middle of the road
b   Be prepared to slow down
c   Accelerate around them
d   Signal right

## Question 6.32

Mark two answers
You are approaching a roundabout. There are horses just ahead of you. You should

a   be prepared to stop
b   treat them like any other vehicle
c   give them plenty of room
d   accelerate past as quickly as possible
e   sound your horn as a warning

## Question 6.33

Mark three answers
Which THREE should you do when passing sheep on a road?

a   Allow plenty of room
b   Go very slowly
c   Pass quickly but quietly
d   Be ready to stop
e   Briefly sound your horn

## Question 6.34

Mark one answer
At night you see a pedestrian wearing reflective clothing and carrying a bright red light. What does this mean?

a   You are approaching roadworks
b   You are approaching an organised walk
c   You are approaching a slow-moving vehicle
d   You are approaching an accident black spot

## Question 6.35

Mark one answer

As you approach a pelican crossing the lights change to green. Elderly people are halfway across. You should

a   wave them to cross as quickly as they can

b   rev your engine to make them hurry

c   flash your lights in case they have not heard you

d   wait because they will take longer to cross

## Question 6.36

Mark one answer

There are flashing amber lights under a school warning sign. What action should you take?

a   Reduce speed until you are clear of the area

b   Keep up your speed and sound the horn

c   Increase your speed to clear the area quickly

d   Wait at the lights until they change to green

## Question 6.37

Mark one answer

Which of the following types of crossing can detect when people are on them?

a   Pelican

b   Toucan

c   Zebra

d   Puffin

## Question 6.38

Mark one answer

You are approaching this crossing. You should

a   prepare to slow down and stop

b   stop and wave the pedestrians across

c   speed up and pass by quickly

d   drive on unless the pedestrians step out

## Question 6.39

Mark one answer
You see a pedestrian with a dog. The dog has a bright orange lead and collar. This especially warns you that the pedestrian is

a  elderly
b  dog training
c  colour blind
d  deaf

## Question 6.40

Mark one answer
These road markings must be kept clear to allow

a  school children to be dropped off
b  for teachers to park
c  school children to be picked up
d  a clear view of the crossing area

## Question 6.41

Mark one answer
You must not stop on these road markings because you may obstruct

a  children's view of the crossing area
b  teachers access to the school
c  delivery vehicles access to the school
d  emergency vehicles access to the school

## Question 6.42

Mark one answer
Where would you see this sign?

a  Near a school crossing
b  At a playground entrance
c  On a school bus
d  At a 'pedestrians only' area

## Question 6.43

Mark one answer

The left-hand pavement is closed due to street repairs. What should you do?

a  Watch out for pedestrians walking in the road

b  Use your right-hand mirror more often

c  Speed up to get past the road works quicker

d  Position close to the left-hand kerb

## Question 6.44

Mark one answer

You are following a motorcyclist on an uneven road. You should

a  allow less room so you can be seen in their mirrors

b  overtake immediately

c  allow extra room in case they swerve to avoid pot-holes

d  allow the same room as normal because road surfaces do not affect motorcyclists

## Question 6.45

Mark one answer

You are following two cyclists. They approach a roundabout in the left-hand lane. In which direction should you expect the cyclists to go?

a  Left

b  Right

c  Any direction

d  Straight ahead

## Question 6.46

Mark one answer

You are travelling behind a moped. You want to turn left just ahead. You should

a  overtake the moped before the junction

b  pull alongside the moped and stay level until just before the junction

c  sound your horn as a warning and pull in front of the moped

d  stay behind until the moped has passed the junction

## Question 6.47

Mark three answers
Which THREE of the following are hazards motorcyclists present in queues of traffic?

a  Cutting in just in front of you
b  Riding in single file
c  Passing very close to you
d  Riding with their headlight on dipped beam
e  Filtering between the lanes

## Question 6.48

Mark one answer
You see a horse rider as you approach a roundabout. They are signalling right but keeping well to the left. You should

a  proceed as normal
b  keep close to them
c  cut in front of them
d  stay well back

## Question 6.49

Mark one answer
How would you react to drivers who appear to be inexperienced?

a  Sound your horn to warn them of your presence
b  Be patient and prepare for them to react more slowly
c  Flash your headlights to indicate that it is safe for them to proceed
d  Overtake them as soon as possible

## Question 6.50

Mark one answer
You are following a learner driver who stalls at a junction. You should

a  be patient as you expect them to make mistakes
b  stay very close behind and flash your headlights
c  start to rev your engine if they take too long to restart
d  immediately steer around them and drive on

## Question 6.51

Mark one answer
You are on a country road. What should you expect to see coming towards you on YOUR side of the road?

a   Motorcycles
b   Bicycles
c   Pedestrians
d   Horse riders

## Question 6.52

Mark one answer
You are turning left into a side road. Pedestrians are crossing the road near the junction. You must

a   wave them on
b   sound your horn
c   switch on your hazard lights
d   wait for them to cross

## Question 6.53

Mark one answer
You are following a car driven by an elderly driver. You should

a   expect the driver to drive badly
b   flash your lights and overtake
c   be aware that the driver's reactions may not be as fast as yours
d   stay very close behind but be careful

## Question 6.54

Mark one answer
You are following a cyclist. You wish to turn left just ahead. You should

a   overtake the cyclist before the junction
b   pull alongside the cyclist and stay level until after the junction
c   hold back until the cyclist has passed the junction
d   go around the cyclist on the junction

## Question 6.55

Mark one answer
A horse rider is in the left-hand lane approaching a roundabout. You should expect the rider to

a   go in any direction
b   turn right
c   turn left
d   go ahead

## Question 6.56

Mark one answer
You have just passed your test. How can you decrease your risk of accidents on the motorway?

a   By keeping up with the car in front
b   By never going over 40mph
c   By staying only in the left-hand lane
d   By taking further training

## Question 6.57

Mark one answer
Powered vehicles used by disabled people are small and hard to see. How do they give early warning when on a dual carriageway?

a   They will have a flashing red light
b   They will have a flashing green light
c   They will have a flashing blue light
d   They will have a flashing amber light

## Question 6.58

Mark one answer
You should never attempt to overtake a cyclist

a   just before you turn left
b   on a left-hand bend
c   on a one-way street
d   on a dual carriageway

## Question 6.59

Mark one answer
Ahead of you there is a moving vehicle with a flashing amber beacon. This means it is

a   slow-moving
b   broken down
c   a doctor's car
d   a school-crossing patrol

## Question 6.60

Mark one answer
You want to reverse into a side road. You are not sure that the area behind your car is clear. What should you do?

a   Look through the rear window only
b   Get out and check
c   Check the mirrors only
d   Carry on, assuming it is clear

## Question 6.61

Mark one answer
You are about to reverse into a side road. A pedestrian wishes to cross behind you. You should

a  wave to the pedestrian to stop
b  give way to the pedestrian
c  wave to the pedestrian to cross
d  reverse before the pedestrian starts to cross

## Question 6.62

Mark one answer
Who is especially in danger of not being seen as you reverse your car?

a  Motorcyclists
b  Car drivers
c  Cyclists
d  Children

## Question 6.63

Mark one answer
You are reversing around a corner when you notice a pedestrian walking behind you. What should you do?

a  Slow down and wave the pedestrian across
b  Continue reversing and steer round the pedestrian
c  Stop and give way
d  Continue reversing and sound your horn

## Question 6.64

Mark one answer
You want to turn right from a junction but your view is restricted by parked vehicles. What should you do?

a  Move out quickly, but be prepared to stop
b  Sound your horn and pull out if there is no reply
c  Stop, then move slowly forward until you have a clear view
d  Stop, get out and look along the main road to check

## Question 6.65

Mark one answer
You are at the front of a queue of traffic waiting to turn right into a side road. Why is it important to check your right mirror just before turning?

a   To look for pedestrians about to cross
b   To check for overtaking vehicles
c   To make sure the side road is clear
d   To check for emerging traffic

## Question 6.66

Mark one answer
What must a driver do at a pelican crossing when the amber light is flashing?

a   Signal the pedestrian to cross
b   Always wait for the green light before proceeding
c   Give way to any pedestrians on the crossing
d   Wait for the red-and-amber light before proceeding

## Question 6.67

Mark two answers
You have stopped at a pelican crossing. A disabled person is crossing slowly in front of you. The lights have now changed to green. You should

a   allow the person to cross
b   drive in front of the person
c   drive behind the person
d   sound your horn
e   be patient
f   edge forward slowly

## Question 6.68

Mark one answer
You are driving past parked cars. You notice a wheel of a bicycle sticking out between them. What should you do?

a   Accelerate past quickly and sound your horn
b   Slow down and wave the cyclist across
c   Brake sharply and flash your headlights
d   Slow down and be prepared to stop for a cyclist

## Question 6.69

Mark one answer
You are driving past a line of parked cars. You notice a ball bouncing out into the road ahead. What should you do?

a Continue driving at the same speed and sound your horn
b Continue driving at the same speed and flash your headlights
c Slow down and be prepared to stop for children
d Stop and wave the children across to fetch their ball

## Question 6.70

Mark one answer
You want to turn right from a main road into a side road. Just before turning you should

a cancel your right-turn signal
b select first gear
c check for traffic overtaking on your right
d stop and set the handbrake

## Question 6.71

Mark one answer
You are driving in slow-moving queues of traffic. Just before changing lane you should

a sound the horn
b look for motorcyclists filtering through the traffic
c give a 'slowing down' arm signal
d change down to first gear

## Question 6.72

Mark one answer
You are driving in town. There is a bus at the bus stop on the other side of the road. Why should you be careful?

a The bus may have broken down
b Pedestrians may come from behind the bus
c The bus may move off suddenly
d The bus may remain stationary

## Question 6.73

Mark one answer
How should you overtake horse riders?

a Drive up close and overtake as soon as possible
b Speed is not important but allow plenty of room
c Use your horn just once to warn them
d Drive slowly and leave plenty of room

## Question 6.74

Mark one answer
A friend wants to teach you to drive a car. They must

a  be over 21 and have held a full licence for at least two years
b  be over 18 and hold an advanced driver's certificate
c  be over 18 and have fully comprehensive insurance
d  be over 21 and have held a full licence for at least three years

## Question 6.75

Mark one answer
You are dazzled at night by a vehicle behind you. You should

a  set your mirror to anti dazzle
b  set your mirror to dazzle the other driver
c  brake sharply to a stop
d  switch your rear lights on and off

## Question 6.76

Mark one answer
You have a collision while your car is moving. What is the first thing you must do?

a  Stop only if there are injured people
b  Call the emergency services
c  Stop at the scene of the accident
d  Call your insurance company

## Question 6.77

Mark one answer
Yellow zig zag lines on the road outside schools mean

**/\\-SCHOOL KEEP CLEAR-/\\**

a  sound your horn to alert other road users
b  stop to allow children to cross
c  you must not wait or park on these lines
d  you must not drive over these lines

## Question 6.78

Mark one answer
What do these road markings outside a school mean?

**W-SCHOOL KEEP CLEAR-W**

a   You may park here if you are a teacher
b   Sound your horn before parking
c   When parking use your hazard warning lights
d   You must not wait or park your vehicle here

## Question 6.79

Mark one answer
You are driving on a main road. You intend to turn right into a side road. Just before turning you should

a   adjust your interior mirror
b   flash your headlamps
c   steer over to the left
d   check for traffic overtaking on your right

## Question 6.80

Mark one answer
Why should you allow extra room when overtaking a motorcyclist on a windy day?

a   The rider may turn off suddenly to get out of the wind
b   The rider may be blown across in front of you
c   The rider may stop suddenly
d   The rider may be travelling faster than normal

## Question 6.81

Mark one answer
Which age group of drivers is most likely to be involved in a road accident?

a   36 to 45-year-olds
b   55-year-olds and over
c   46 to 55-year-olds
d   17 to 25-year-olds

## Question 6.82

Mark one answer
You are driving towards a zebra crossing. Waiting to cross is a person in a wheelchair. You should

a   continue on your way
b   wave to the person to cross
c   wave to the person to wait
d   be prepared to stop

## Question 6.83

Mark one answer
Where in particular should you look out
for motorcyclists?

a   In a filling station
b   At a road junction
c   Near a service area
d   When entering a car park

## Question 6.84

Mark one answer
The road outside this school is marked
with yellow zigzag lines. What do these
lines mean?

a   You may park on the lines when
    dropping off schoolchildren
b   You may park on the lines when
    picking schoolchildren up
c   You must not wait or park your
    vehicle here at all
d   You must stay with your vehicle if you
    park here

## Question 6.85

Mark one answer
Where should you take particular care to
look out for motorcyclists and cyclists?

a   On dual carriageways
b   At junctions
c   At zebra crossings
d   On one-way streets

## Answers and explanations

6.1   <u>d</u> Red triangles give warnings, in this case of people walking along the road. 'c' is a warning of a pedestrian crossing.

6.2   <u>d</u>

6.3   <u>c</u>

6.4   <u>c</u>

6.5   <u>b</u>

6.6   <u>d</u>

6.7   <u>d</u>

6.8   <u>a, d</u>

6.9   <u>b</u>

6.10   <u>c</u>

6.11   <u>d</u>

6.12   <u>a</u>

6.13   <u>d</u>

6.14   <u>d</u>

6.15   <u>b</u>

6.16   <u>d</u> The ability to judge speed tends to deteriorate as you get older.

6.17   <u>b</u>

6.18   <u>d</u>

6.19   <u>d</u>

6.20   <u>c</u> 'c' is the answer required, but you should also be aware that cyclists can be unpredictable.

6.21   <u>a, c</u>
Motorcycles and bicycles can easily swerve and you need to allow them extra room.

6.22   <u>c</u>

6.23   <u>c</u>

6.24   <u>a</u>

6.25   <u>d</u>

6.26   <u>c</u>

6.27   <u>d</u>

6.28   <u>a, b, c</u>

6.29   <u>c</u>

6.30   <u>b</u>

6.31   <u>b</u> Horses and their riders can be unpredictable so 'b' is the safest first action.

6.32   <u>a, c</u>

6.33   <u>a, b, d</u>

6.34   <u>b</u>

6.35   <u>d</u>

6.36   <u>a</u>

6.37   <u>d</u>

6.38   <u>a</u>

6.39   <u>d</u>

6.40   <u>d</u> You must not park on these yellow zig zag lines, not even to drop off or pick up children.

6.41   <u>a</u>

6.42   <u>c</u>

6.43   <u>a</u> Remember that pedestrians walking in the road will have their backs to you, so give them plenty of space.

6.44   <u>c</u>

6.45   <u>c</u>

6.46   <u>d</u>

6.47   <u>a, c, e</u>
Check your door mirrors, especially before moving forwards or changing lanes.

6.48   <u>d</u>

6.49   <u>b</u>

6.50   <u>a</u>

6.51   <u>c</u> Pedestrians are the most likely to expect as country roads often have no pavements and pedestrians are advised to walk on the right so that they can see oncoming traffic on their side of the road. However, you should always expect the unexpected when driving.

6.52 d When you turn into a side road pedestrians who are already crossing have priority so you must give way.

6.53 c

6.54 c As the question states you are turning left JUST ahead, you have no time to overtake the cyclist safely which is why 'c' is correct.

6.55 a

6.56 d In many countries motorway tuition is compulsory. Motorway driving contains many new challenges and tuition is strongly recommended. Speak to your instructor for advice.

6.57 d

6.58 a The word 'NEVER' makes 'a' correct.

6.59 a

6.60 b

6.61 b

6.62 d Children are small and you may not be able to see them through your rear windscreen.

6.63 c

6.64 c You cannot turn right until you can see it is safe to do so. You should stop and then edge slowly forwards until you can see clearly to the left and right.

6.65 b

6.66 c

6.67 a, e

6.68 d

6.69 c

6.70 c Use your right-door mirror and look particularly for motorcyclists.

6.71 b

6.72 b

6.73 d

6.74 d

6.75 a

6.76 c

6.77 c

6.78 d

6.79 d

6.80 b

6.81 d

6.82 d

6.83 b

6.84 c

6.85 b

# Theory Test Questions for Car Drivers

## 2004–2005

## Section 7

# Other types of vehicle

## Question 7.1

Mark one answer
The road is wet. Why might a motorcyclist steer round drain covers on a bend?

a   To avoid puncturing the tyres on the edge of the drain covers

b   To prevent the motorcycle sliding on the metal drain covers

c   To help judge the bend using the drain covers as marker points

d   To avoid splashing pedestrians on the pavement

## Question 7.2

Mark one answer
You are about to overtake a slow-moving motorcyclist. Which one of these signs would make you take special care?

a         b

c         d

## Question 7.3

Mark one answer
You are waiting to emerge left from a minor road. A large vehicle is approaching from the right. You have time to turn, but you should wait. Why?

a   The large vehicle can easily hide an overtaking vehicle

b   The large vehicle can turn suddenly

c   The large vehicle is difficult to steer in a straight line

d   The large vehicle can easily hide vehicles from the left

## Question 7.4

Mark one answer
You are following a long vehicle. It approaches a crossroads and signals left, but moves out to the right. You should

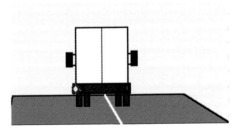

a   get closer in order to pass it quickly

b   stay well back and give it room

c   assume the signal is wrong and it is really turning right

d   overtake as it starts to slow down

## Question 7.5

Mark one answer
You are following a long vehicle approaching a crossroads. The driver signals right but moves close to the left-hand kerb. What should you do?

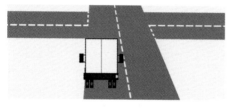

a Warn the driver of the wrong signal
b Wait behind the long vehicle
c Report the driver to the police
d Overtake on the right-hand side

## Question 7.6

Mark one answer
You are approaching a mini-roundabout. The long vehicle in front is signalling left but positioned over to the right. You should

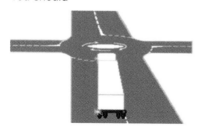

a sound your horn
b overtake on the left
c follow the same course as the lorry
d keep well back

## Question 7.7

Mark one answer
Before overtaking a large vehicle you should keep well back. Why is this?

a To give acceleration space to overtake quickly on blind bends
b To get the best view of the road ahead
c To leave a gap in case the vehicle stops and rolls back
d To offer other drivers a safe gap if they want to overtake you

## Question 7.8

Mark one answer
Why is passing a lorry more risky than passing a car?

a Lorries are longer than cars
b Lorries may suddenly pull up
c The brakes of lorries are not as good
d Lorries climb hills more slowly

## Question 7.9

Mark two answers
You are travelling behind a bus that pulls up at a bus stop. What should you do?

a Accelerate past the bus sounding your horn
b Watch carefully for pedestrians
c Be ready to give way to the bus
d Pull in closely behind the bus

## Question 7.10

Mark one answer
When you approach a bus signalling to move off from a bus stop you should

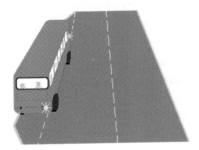

a   get past before it moves
b   allow it to pull away, if it is safe
     to do so
c   flash your headlights as you approach
d   signal left and wave the bus on

## Question 7.11

Mark one answer
Which of these vehicles is LEAST likely to be affected by crosswinds?

a   Cyclists
b   Motorcyclists
c   High-sided vehicles
d   Cars

## Question 7.12

Mark one answer
You are following a large lorry on a wet road. Spray makes it difficult to see. You should

a   drop back until you can see better
b   put your headlights on full beam
c   keep close to the lorry, away from
     the spray
d   speed up and overtake quickly

## Question 7.13

Mark one answer
Some two-way roads are divided into three lanes. Why are these particularly dangerous?

a   Traffic in both directions can use the
     middle lane to overtake
b   Traffic can travel faster in poor
     weather conditions
c   Traffic can overtake on the left
d   Traffic uses the middle lane for
     emergencies only

## Question 7.14

Mark one answer
What should you do as you approach this lorry?

a   Slow down and be prepared to wait
b   Make the lorry wait for you
c   Flash your lights at the lorry
d   Move to the right-hand side of the road

## Question 7.15

Mark one answer
You are following a large articulated vehicle. It is going to turn left into a narrow road. What action should you take?

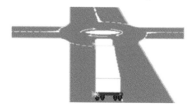

a   Move out and overtake on the right
b   Pass on the left as the vehicle moves out
c   Be prepared to stop behind
d   Overtake quickly before the lorry moves out

## Question 7.16

Mark one answer
You keep well back while waiting to overtake a large vehicle. A car fills the gap. You should

a   sound your horn
b   drop back further
c   flash your headlights
d   start to overtake

## Question 7.17

Mark one answer
At a junction you see this signal. It means

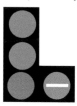

a   cars must stop
b   trams must stop
c   both trams and cars must stop
d   both trams and cars can continue

## Question 7.18

Mark one answer

You are following a large vehicle approaching crossroads. The driver signals to turn left. What should you do?

a   Overtake if you can leave plenty of room

b   Overtake only if there are no oncoming vehicles

c   Do not overtake until the vehicle begins to turn

d   Do not overtake when at or approaching a junction

## Question 7.19

Mark one answer

You are following a long lorry. The driver signals to turn left into a narrow road. What should you do?

a   Overtake on the left before the lorry reaches the junction

b   Overtake on the right as soon as the lorry slows down

c   Do not overtake unless you can see there is no oncoming traffic

d   Do not overtake, stay well back and be prepared to stop

## Question 7.20

Mark one answer

You wish to overtake a long, slow-moving vehicle on a busy road. You should

a   follow it closely and keep moving out to see the road ahead

b   flash your headlights for the oncoming traffic to give way

c   stay behind until the driver waves you past

d   keep well back until you can see that it is clear

## Question 7.21

Mark one answer

It is very windy. You are behind a motorcyclist who is overtaking a high-sided vehicle. What should you do?

a   Overtake the motorcyclist immediately

b   Keep well back

c   Stay level with the motorcyclist

d   Keep close to the motorcyclist

## Question 7.22

Mark one answer

It is very windy. You are about to overtake a motorcyclist. You should

a   overtake slowly

b   allow extra room

c   sound your horn

d   keep close as you pass

## Question 7.23

Mark one answer
You are towing a caravan. Which is the safest type of rear-view mirror to use?

a   Interior wide-angle-view mirror
b   Extended-arm side mirrors
c   Ordinary door mirrors
d   Ordinary interior mirror

## Question 7.24

Mark one answer
You are driving downhill. There is a car parked on the other side of the road. Large, slow lorries are coming towards you. You should

a   keep going because you have the right of way
b   slow down and give way
c   speed up and get past quickly
d   pull over on the right behind the parked car

## Question 7.25

Mark two answers
You are driving in town. Ahead of you a bus is at a bus stop. Which TWO of the following should you do?

a   Be prepared to give way if the bus suddenly moves off
b   Continue at the same speed but sound your horn as a warning
c   Watch carefully for the sudden appearance of pedestrians
d   Pass the bus as quickly as you possibly can

## Question 7.26

Mark two answers
You are driving in heavy traffic on a wet road. Spray makes it difficult to be seen. You should use your

a   full beam headlights
b   rear fog lights if visibility is less than 100 metres (328 feet)
c   rear fog lights if visibility is more than 100 metres (328 feet)
d   dipped headlights
e   side lights only

## Question 7.27

Mark one answer
You are driving along this road. What should you be prepared to do?

a   Sound your horn and continue
b   Slow down and give way
c   Report the driver to the police
d   Squeeze through the gap

## Question 7.28

Mark one answer
You are on a wet motorway with surface spray. You should use

a   hazard flashers
b   dipped headlights
c   rear fog lights
d   sidelights

## Question 7.29

Mark one answer
As a driver why should you be more careful where trams operate?

a   Because they do not have a horn
b   Because they do not stop for cars
c   Because they do not have lights
d   Because they cannot steer to avoid you

### Answers and explanations

7.1   b Water on metal is a dangerous combination, especially for a two-wheeled vehicle.

7.2   a The motorcyclist may wobble as you pass by in a windy situation.

7.3   a

7.4   b Long vehicles require more space to turn and often need to position for this.

7.5   b

7.6   d

7.7   b

7.8   a Overtaking takes time, so the longer the vehicle you overtake the greater the danger, as you will take longer to pass it.

7.9   b, c

7.10   b This helps traffic flow without giving confusing signals.

7.11   d Of the four mentioned, cars are by far the most stable and least affected by crosswinds.

7.12   a

7.13   a

7.14   a

7.15   c The large articulated vehicle may need to position to the right in order to turn left into the narrow road.

7.16   b

7.17   b

7.18   d

7.19   d

7.20   d

7.21   b Let the motorcyclist complete the overtake before even thinking about following.

7.22   b Motorcycles may have problems with strong crosswinds.

7.23   b

7.24   b

7.25   a, c

7.26   b, d

7.27   b

7.28   b

7.29   d

# Theory Test Questions for Car Drivers

2004–2005

Section 8     Vehicle handling

## Question 8.1

Mark one answer
You are following a vehicle at a safe distance on a wet road. Another driver overtakes you and pulls into the gap you have left. What should you do?

a   Flash your headlights as a warning
b   Try to overtake safely as soon as you can
c   Drop back to regain a safe distance
d   Stay close to the other vehicle until it moves on

## Question 8.2

Mark three answers
In which THREE of these situations may you overtake another vehicle on the left?

a   When you are in a one-way street
b   When approaching a motorway slip road where you will be turning off
c   When the vehicle in front is signalling to turn right
d   When a slower vehicle is travelling in the right-hand lane of a dual carriageway
e   In slow-moving traffic queues when traffic in the right-hand lane is moving more slowly

## Question 8.3

Mark one answer
You are travelling in very heavy rain. Your overall stopping distance is likely to be

a   doubled
b   halved
c   up to ten times greater
d   no different

## Question 8.4

Mark two answers
Which TWO of the following are correct? When overtaking at night you should

a   wait until a bend so that you can see the oncoming headlights
b   sound your horn twice before moving out
c   be careful because you can see less
d   beware of bends in the road ahead
e   put headlights on full beam

## Question 8.5

Mark one answer
When may you wait in a box junction?

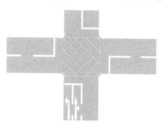

a When you are stationary in a queue of traffic
b When approaching a pelican crossing
c When approaching a zebra crossing
d When oncoming traffic prevents you turning right

## Question 8.6

Mark one answer
Which of these plates normally appear with this road sign?

| Humps for ½ mile | HumpBridge |
|------|------|
| a | b |

| Low Bridge | Soft Verge |
|------|------|
| c | d |

## Question 8.7

Mark three answers
Areas reserved for trams may have

a metal studs around them
b white line markings
c zig zag markings
d a different coloured surface
e yellow hatch markings
f a different surface texture

## Question 8.8

Mark one answer
Traffic calming measures are used to

a stop road rage
b help overtaking
c slow traffic down
d help parking

## Question 8.9

Mark one answer
Why should you always reduce your speed when travelling in fog?

a Because the brakes do not work as well
b Because you could be dazzled by other people's fog lights
c Because the engine is colder
d Because it is more difficult to see events ahead

## Question 8.10

<u>Mark one answer</u>
You are on a motorway in fog. The left-hand edge of the motorway can be identified by reflective studs. What colour are they?

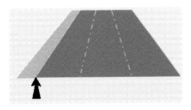

a   Green
b   Amber
c   Red
d   White

## Question 8.11

<u>Mark two answers</u>
A rumble device is designed to

a   give directions
b   prevent cattle escaping
c   alert you to low tyre pressure
d   alert you to a hazard
e   encourage you to reduce speed

## Question 8.12

<u>Mark one answer</u>
You are on a narrow road at night. A slower-moving vehicle ahead has been signalling right for some time. What should you do?

a   Overtake on the left
b   Flash your headlights before overtaking
c   Signal right and sound your horn
d   Wait for the signal to be cancelled before overtaking

## Question 8.13

<u>Mark one answer</u>
Why should you test your brakes after this hazard?

a   Because you will be on a slippery road
b   Because your brakes will be soaking wet
c   Because you will have gone down a long hill
d   Because you will have just crossed a long bridge

## Question 8.14

Mark one answer

You have to make a journey in foggy conditions. You should

a follow other vehicles' tail lights closely
b avoid using dipped headlights
c leave plenty of time for your journey
d keep two seconds behind other vehicles

## Question 8.15

Mark one answer

You are overtaking a car at night. You must be sure that

a you flash your headlights before overtaking
b you select a higher gear
c you have switched your lights to full beam before overtaking
d you do not dazzle other road users

## Question 8.16

Mark one answer

You see a vehicle coming towards you on a single track road. You should

a go back to the main road
b do an emergency stop
c stop at a passing place
d put on your hazard warning lights

## Question 8.17

Mark one answer

You are on a road which has speed humps. A driver in front is travelling slower than you. You should

a sound your horn
b overtake as soon as you can
c flash your headlights
d slow down and stay behind

## Question 8.18

Mark one answer

You are following other vehicles in fog with your lights on. How else can you reduce the chances of being involved in an accident?

a Keep close to the vehicle in front
b Use your main beam instead of dipped headlights
c Keep together with the faster vehicles
d Reduce your speed and increase the gap

## Question 8.19

Mark one answer
You see these markings on the road.
Why are they there?

a   To show a safe distance between
    vehicles
b   To keep the area clear of traffic
c   To make you aware of your speed
d   To warn you to change direction

## Question 8.20

Mark one answer
When MUST you use dipped headlights
during the day?

a   All the time
b   Along narrow streets
c   In poor visibility
d   When parking

## Question 8.21

Mark two answers
What are TWO main reasons why
coasting downhill is wrong?

a   Fuel consumption will be higher
b   The vehicle will pick up speed
c   It puts more wear and tear on the
    tyres
d   You have less braking and steering
    control
e   It damages the engine

## Question 8.22

Mark two answers
Hills can affect the performance of your
vehicle. Which TWO apply when driving
up steep hills?

a   Higher gears will pull better
b   You will slow down sooner
c   Overtaking will be easier
d   The engine will work harder
e   The steering will feel heavier

## Question 8.23

Mark one answer
Why is coasting wrong?

a   It will cause the car to skid
b   It will make the engine stall
c   The engine will run faster
d   There is no engine braking

## Question 8.24

Mark one answer
You are driving on the motorway in windy conditions. When passing high-sided vehicles you should

a  increase your speed
b  be wary of a sudden gust
c  drive alongside very closely
d  expect normal conditions

## Question 8.25

Mark one answer
To correct a rear-wheel skid you should

a  not steer at all
b  steer away from it
c  steer into it
d  apply your handbrake

## Question 8.26

Mark two answers
You have to make a journey in fog. What are the TWO most important things you should do before you set out?

a  Top up the radiator with antifreeze
b  Make sure that you have a warning triangle in the vehicle
c  Check that your lights are working
d  Check the battery
e  Make sure that the windows are clean

## Question 8.27

Mark one answer
You are driving in fog. Why should you keep well back from the vehicle in front?

a  In case it changes direction suddenly
b  In case its fog lights dazzle you
c  In case it stops suddenly
d  In case its brake lights dazzle you

## Question 8.28

Mark one answer
You should switch your rear fog lights on when visibility drops below

a  your overall stopping distance
b  ten car lengths
c  200 metres (656 feet)
d  100 metres (328 feet)

## Question 8.29

Mark one answer
While driving, the fog clears and you can see more clearly. You must remember to

a  switch off the fog lights
b  reduce your speed
c  switch off the demister
d  close any open windows

## Question 8.30

Mark one answer
You have to park on the road in fog.
You should

a   leave sidelights on
b   leave dipped headlights and fog lights
    on
c   leave dipped headlights on
d   leave main beam headlights on

## Question 8.31

Mark one answer
On a foggy day you unavoidably have to
park your car on the road. You should

a   leave your headlights on
b   leave your fog lights on
c   leave your sidelights on
d   leave your hazard lights on

## Question 8.32

Mark one answer
You are travelling at night. You are
dazzled by headlights coming towards
you. You should

a   pull down your sun visor
b   slow down or stop
c   switch on your main beam headlights
d   put your hand over your eyes

## Question 8.33

Mark four answers
Which of the following may apply when
dealing with this hazard?

a   It could be more difficult in winter
b   Use a low gear and drive slowly
c   Use a high gear to prevent wheelspin
d   Test your brakes afterwards
e   Always switch on fog lamps
f   There may be a depth gauge

## Question 8.34

Mark one answer
Front fog lights may be used only if

a   visibility is seriously reduced
b   they are fitted above the bumper
c   they are not as bright as the
    headlights
d   an audible warning device is used

## Question 8.35

Mark one answer
Front fog lights may be used only if

a   your headlights are not working
b   they are operated with rear fog lights
c   they were fitted by the vehicle
    manufacturer
d   visibility is seriously reduced

## Question 8.36

Mark one answer
You are driving with your front fog lights switched on. Earlier fog has now cleared. What should you do?

a   Leave them on if other drivers have
    their lights on
b   Switch them off as long as visibility
    remains good
c   Flash them to warn oncoming traffic
    that it is foggy
d   Drive with them on instead of your
    headlights

## Question 8.37

Mark one answer
Front fog lights should be used only when

a   travelling in very light rain
b   visibility is seriously reduced
c   daylight is fading
d   driving after midnight

## Question 8.38 NI Exempt

Mark two answers
Why is it dangerous to leave rear fog lights on when they are not needed?

a   Brake lights are less clear
b   Following drivers can be dazzled
c   Electrical systems could be
    overloaded
d   Direction indicators may not work
    properly
e   The battery could fail

## Question 8.39 NI Exempt

Mark two answers
You are driving on a clear dry night with your rear fog lights switched on. This may

a   reduce glare from the road surface
b   make other drivers think you are
    braking
c   give a better view of the road ahead
d   dazzle following drivers
e   help your indicators to be seen more
    clearly

133

## Question 8.40

Mark one answer
You have just driven out of fog. Visibility is now good. You MUST

a   switch off all your fog lights
b   keep your rear fog lights on
c   keep your front fog lights on
d   leave fog lights on in case fog returns

## Question 8.41 NI Exempt

Mark three answers
You forget to switch off your rear fog lights when the fog has cleared. This may

a   dazzle other road users
b   reduce battery life
c   cause brake lights to be less clear
d   be breaking the law
e   seriously affect engine power

## Question 8.42 NI Exempt

Mark one answer
You have been driving in thick fog which has now cleared. You must switch OFF your rear fog lights because

a   they use a lot of power from the battery
b   they make your brake lights less clear
c   they will cause dazzle in your rear view mirrors
d   they may not be properly adjusted

## Question 8.43

Mark one answer
Front fog lights should be used

a   when visibility is reduced to 100 metres (328 feet)
b   as a warning to oncoming traffic
c   when driving during the hours of darkness
d   in any conditions and at any time

## Question 8.44

Mark one answer
Using rear fog lights in clear daylight will

a   be useful when towing a trailer
b   give extra protection
c   dazzle other drivers
d   make following drivers keep back

## Question 8.45

Mark one answer
Using front fog lights in clear daylight will

a   flatten the battery
b   dazzle other drivers
c   improve your visibility
d   increase your awareness

## Question 8.46

Mark one answer
You may use front fog lights with headlights ONLY when visibility is reduced to less than

a  100 metres (328 feet)
b  200 metres (656 feet)
c  300 metres (984 feet)
d  400 metres (1312 feet)

## Question 8.47

Mark one answer
You may drive with front fog lights switched-on

a  when visibility is less than 100 metres (328 feet)
b  at any time to be noticed
c  instead of headlights on high speed roads
d  when dazzled by the lights of oncoming vehicles

## Question 8.48

Mark one answer
Chains can be fitted to your wheels to help prevent

a  damage to the road surface
b  wear to the tyres
c  skidding in deep snow
d  the brakes locking

## Question 8.49

Mark one answer
Pressing the clutch pedal down or rolling in neutral for too long while driving will

a  use more fuel
b  cause the engine to overheat
c  reduce your control
d  improve tyre wear

## Question 8.50

Mark one answer
How can you use the engine of your vehicle to control your speed?

a  By changing to a lower gear
b  By selecting reverse gear
c  By changing to a higher gear
d  By selecting neutral

## Question 8.51

Mark one answer
You are driving down a steep hill. Why could keeping the clutch down or selecting neutral for too long be dangerous?

a   Fuel consumption will be higher
b   Your vehicle will pick up speed
c   It will damage the engine
d   It will wear tyres out more quickly

## Question 8.52

Mark one answer
Why could keeping the clutch down or selecting neutral for long periods of time be dangerous?

a   Fuel spillage will occur
b   Engine damage may be caused
c   You will have less steering and braking control
d   It will wear tyres out more quickly

## Question 8.53

Mark one answer
You are driving on an icy road. What distance should you drive from the car in front?

a   Four times the normal distance
b   Six times the normal distance
c   Eight times the normal distance
d   Ten times the normal distance

## Question 8.54

Mark one answer
You are on a well-lit motorway at night. You must

a   use only your sidelights
b   always use your headlights
c   always use rear fog lights
d   use headlights only in bad weather

## Question 8.55

Mark one answer
You are on a motorway at night with other vehicles just ahead of you. Which lights should you have on?

a   Front fog lights
b   Main beam headlights
c   Sidelights only
d   Dipped headlights

## Question 8.56

Mark three answers
Which THREE of the following will affect your stopping distance?

a   How fast you are going
b   The tyres on your vehicle
c   The time of day
d   The weather
e   The street lighting

## Question 8.57

Mark one answer

You are on a motorway at night. You MUST have your headlights switched on unless

a  there are vehicles close in front of you
b  you are travelling below 50mph
c  the motorway is lit
d  your vehicle is broken down on the hard shoulder

## Question 8.58

Mark one answer

You will feel the effects of engine braking when you

a  only use the handbrake
b  only use neutral
c  change to a lower gear
d  change to a higher gear

## Question 8.59

Mark one answer

Daytime visibility is poor but not seriously reduced. You should switch on

a  headlights and fog lights
b  front fog lights
c  dipped headlights
d  rear fog lights

## Question 8.60

Mark one answer

Why are vehicles fitted with rear fog lights?

a  To be seen when driving at high speed
b  To use if broken down in a dangerous position
c  To make them more visible in thick fog
d  To warn drivers following closely to drop back

## Question 8.61

Mark one answer

While you are driving in fog, it becomes necessary to use front fog lights. You should

a  only turn them on in heavy traffic conditions
b  remember not to use them on motorways
c  only use them on dual carriageways
d  remember to switch them off as visibility improves

## Question 8.62

When snow is falling heavily you should

a  only drive with your hazard lights on
b  not drive unless you have a mobile phone
c  only drive when your journey is short
d  not drive unless it is essential

## Question 8.63

You are driving down a long, steep hill. You suddenly notice your brakes are not working as well as normal. What is the usual cause of this?

a  The brakes overheating
b  Air in the brake fluid
c  Oil on the brakes
d  Badly adjusted brakes

## Answers and explanations

8.1    c This may feel irritating, particularly if the circumstance is repeated several times. However, it is safest and, in reality, causes no delay.

8.2    a, c, e

8.3    a

8.4    c, d

8.5    d You may wait in a box junction if your exit is clear but oncoming traffic prevents you from turning right.

8.6    a

8.7    b, d, f

8.8    c

8.9    d Everybody knows this but an alarming number of people don't put the knowledge into practice. Accidents happen as a result.

8.10   c Red reflective studs separate the left-hand lane and the hard shoulder.

8.11   d, e
       A rumble device is normally raised strips or markings on the surface of the road.

8.12   d

8.13   b After driving through water your brakes will be wet, and wet brakes are inefficient.

8.14   c The Highway Code advises you to allow more time for your journey in foggy conditions. However, always ask yourself if the journey really is necessary.

8.15    d You may need to switch to full-
        beam headlights as you
        overtake, but not before.

8.16    c Bear in mind that single-track
        roads may have passing places
        at long intervals. You may meet
        an oncoming vehicle at a point
        where one of you will need to
        reverse to the previous nearest
        passing point.

8.17    d

8.18    d

8.19    c

8.20    c

8.21    b, d

8.22    b, d

8.23    d You are coasting when you push
        down the clutch, disconnecting
        both engine and gear box.

8.24    b

8.25    c

8.26    c, e
        See and be seen are the two
        most crucial safety aspects of
        driving in fog.

8.27    c If the car in front stops suddenly
        you may run into it if you have
        been driving too close.

8.28    d Remember to switch them off
        when visibility improves.

8.29    a Fog lights should only be used
        where visibility is down to about
        100 metres. Otherwise you risk
        dazzling other drivers.

8.30    a

8.31    c

8.32    b

8.33    a, b, d, f

8.34    a

8.35    d

8.36    b

8.37    b

8.38    a, b

8.39    b, d

8.40    a

8.41    a, c, d

8.42    b

8.43    a

8.44    c Always remember to switch
        off your fog lights as soon as
        visibility improves.

8.45    b

8.46    a

8.47    a

8.48    c

8.49    c

8.50    a On a long, downhill slope
        changing to a lower gear before
        the descent means that you will
        not need to use the footbrake
        the whole time and will not risk
        the brakes overheating.

8.51    b

8.52    c

8.53    d Stopping distances can be up to
        ten times longer in snow and
        ice. Give yourself plenty of time
        to stop.

8.54    b

8.55    d Full-beam headlights would
        dazzle the drivers in front by
        reflecting in their mirrors.

8.56    a, b, d

8.57    d You must use your headlights
        on motorways at nights even if
        the motorway is lit.

8.58    c

8.59    c

8.60  c

8.61  d

8.62  d

8.63  a Selecting a lower gear before descending a long, steep hill, allows the engine to control the speed of the car and helps prevent the brakes overheating. With a lower gear selected, the footbrake can be used when necessary, rather than the whole time.

# Theory Test Questions for Car Drivers

## 2004–2005

## Section 9

# Motorway rules

## Question 9.1

Mark four answers
Which FOUR of these must NOT use motorways?

a  Learner car drivers
b  Motorcycles over 50cc
c  Double-decker buses
d  Farm tractors
e  Horse riders
f  Cyclists

## Question 9.2

Mark four answers
Which FOUR of these must NOT use motorways?

a  Learner car drivers
b  Motorcycles over 50cc
c  Double-decker buses
d  Farm tractors
e  Learner motorcyclists
f  Cyclists

## Question 9.3

Mark one answer
Immediately after joining a motorway you should normally

a  try to overtake
b  re-adjust your mirrors
c  position your vehicle in the centre lane
d  keep in the left lane

## Question 9.4

Mark one answer
When joining a motorway you must always

a  use the hard shoulder
b  stop at the end of the acceleration lane
c  come to a stop before joining the motorway
d  give way to traffic already on the motorway

## Question 9.5

Mark one answer
What is the national speed limit for cars and motorcycles in the centre lane of a three-lane motorway?

a  40mph
b  50mph
c  60mph
d  70mph

## Question 9.6

Mark one answer
What is the national speed limit on motorways for cars and motorcycles?

a  30mph
b  50mph
c  60mph
d  70mph

## Question 9.7

Mark one answer

The left-hand lane on a three-lane motorway is for use by

a any vehicle
b large vehicles only
c emergency vehicles only
d slow vehicles only

## Question 9.8

Mark one answer

What is the right-hand lane used for on a three-lane motorway?

a Emergency vehicles only
b Overtaking
c Vehicles towing trailers
d Coaches only

## Question 9.9

Mark one answer

Which of these is NOT allowed to travel in the right-hand lane of a three-lane motorway?

a A small delivery van
b A motorcycle
c A vehicle towing a trailer
d A motorcycle and side-car

## Question 9.10

Mark two answers

You are travelling on a motorway. You decide you need a rest. You should

a stop on the hard shoulder
b go to a service area
c park on the slip road
d park on the central reservation
e leave at the next exit

## Question 9.11 NI Exempt

Mark one answer

You break down on a motorway. You need to call for help. Why may it be better to use an emergency roadside telephone rather than a mobile phone?

a It connects you to a local garage
b Using a mobile phone will distract other drivers
c It allows easy location by the emergency services
d Mobile phones do not work on motorways

## Question 9.12

Mark one answer
What should you use the hard shoulder of a motorway for?

a  Stopping in an emergency
b  Leaving the motorway
c  Stopping when you are tired
d  Joining the motorway

## Question 9.13

Mark one answer
After a breakdown you need to rejoin the main carriageway of a motorway from the hard shoulder. You should

a  move out onto the carriageway then build up your speed
b  move out onto the carriageway using your hazard lights
c  gain speed on the hard shoulder before moving out onto the carriageway
d  wait on the hard shoulder until someone flashes their headlights at you

## Question 9.14

Mark one answer
A crawler lane on a motorway is found

a  on a steep gradient
b  before a service area
c  before a junction
d  along the hard shoulder

## Question 9.15

Mark one answer
You are driving on a motorway. There are red flashing lights above every lane. You must

a  pull onto the hard shoulder
b  slow down and watch for further signals
c  leave at the next exit
d  stop and wait

## Question 9.16

Mark one answer

You are driving in the right-hand lane on a motorway. You see these overhead signs. This means

a  move to the left and reduce your speed to 50mph
b  there are roadworks 50 metres (55 yards) ahead
c  use the hard shoulder until you have passed the hazard
d  leave the motorway at the next exit

## Question 9.17

Mark one answer

What do these motorway signs show?

a  They are countdown markers to a bridge
b  They are distance markers to the next telephone
c  They are countdown markers to the next exit
d  They warn of a police control ahead

## Question 9.18

Mark one answer

On a motorway the amber reflective studs can be found between

a  the hard shoulder and the carriageway
b  the acceleration lane and the carriageway
c  the central reservation and the carriageway
d  each pair of the lanes

## Question 9.19

Mark one answer

What colour are the reflective studs between the lanes on a motorway?

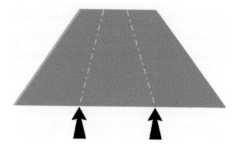

a  Green
b  Amber
c  White
d  Red

145

## Question 9.20

Mark one answer
What colour are the reflective studs between a motorway and its slip road?

a  Amber
b  White
c  Green
d  Red

## Question 9.21

Mark one answer
You are allowed to stop on a motorway when you

a  need to walk and get fresh air
b  wish to pick up hitch hikers
c  are told to do so by flashing red lights
d  need to use a mobile telephone

## Question 9.22

Mark one answer
You have broken down on a motorway. To find the nearest emergency telephone you should always walk

a  with the traffic flow
b  facing oncoming traffic
c  in the direction shown on the marker posts
d  in the direction of the nearest exit

## Question 9.23

Mark one answer
You are travelling along the left lane of a three-lane motorway. Traffic is joining from a slip road. You should

a  race the other vehicles
b  move to another lane
c  maintain a steady speed
d  switch on your hazard flashers

## Question 9.24

Mark one answer
You are joining a motorway. Why is it important to make full use of the slip road?

a  Because there is space available to turn round if you need to
b  To allow you direct access to the overtaking lanes
c  To build up a speed similar to traffic on the motorway
d  Because you can continue on the hard shoulder

## Question 9.25

Mark one answer

How should you use the emergency telephone on a motorway?

a  Stay close to the carriageway
b  Face the oncoming traffic
c  Keep your back to the traffic
d  Stand on the hard shoulder

## Question 9.26

Mark one answer

You are on a motorway. What colour are the reflective studs on the left of the carriageway?

a  Green
b  Red
c  White
d  Amber

## Question 9.27

Mark one answer

On a three-lane motorway which lane should you normally use?

a  Left
b  Right
c  Centre
d  Either the right or centre

## Question 9.28

Mark one answer

A basic rule when on motorways is

a  use the lane that has least traffic
b  keep to the left lane unless overtaking
c  overtake on the side that is clearest
d  try to keep above 50mph to prevent congestion

## Question 9.29

Mark one answer

When going through a contraflow system on a motorway you should

a  ensure that you do not exceed 30mph
b  keep a good distance from the vehicle ahead
c  switch lanes to keep the traffic flowing
d  stay close to the vehicle ahead to reduce queues

## Question 9.30

Mark one answer
You are on a three-lane motorway. There are red reflective studs on your left and white ones to your right. Where are you?

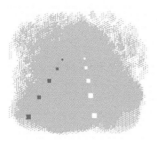

a  In the right-hand lane
b  In the middle lane
c  On the hard shoulder
d  In the left-hand lane

## Question 9.31

Mark three answers
When may you stop on a motorway?

a  If you have to read a map
b  When you are tired and need a rest
c  If red lights show above every lane
d  When told to by the police
e  If your mobile phone rings
f  In an emergency or a breakdown

## Question 9.32

Mark one answer
You are approaching roadworks on a motorway. What should you do?

a  Speed up to clear the area quickly
b  Always use the hard shoulder
c  Obey all speed limits
d  Stay very close to the vehicle in front

## Question 9.33

Mark one answer
On motorways you should never overtake on the left UNLESS

a  you can see well ahead that the hard shoulder is clear
b  the traffic in the right-hand lane is signalling right
c  you warn drivers behind by signalling left
d  there is a queue of slow-moving traffic to your right that is moving slower than you are

## Question 9.34

Mark one answer
You are towing a trailer on a motorway. What is your maximum speed limit?

a  40mph
b  50mph
c  60mph
d  70mph

## Question 9.35

Mark one answer
The left-hand lane of a motorway should be used for

a breakdowns and emergencies only
b overtaking slower traffic in the other lanes
c slow vehicles only
d normal driving

## Question 9.36

Mark one answer
You are driving on a motorway. You have to slow down quickly due to a hazard. You should

a switch on your hazard lights
b switch on your headlights
c sound your horn
d flash your headlights

## Question 9.37

Mark one answer
You get a puncture on the motorway. You manage to get your vehicle onto the hard shoulder. You should

a change the wheel yourself immediately
b use the emergency telephone and call for assistance
c try to wave down another vehicle for help
d only change the wheel if you have a passenger to help you

## Question 9.38

Mark one answer
You are driving on a motorway. By mistake, you go past the exit that you wanted to take. You should

a carefully reverse on the hard shoulder
b carry on to the next exit
c carefully reverse in the left-hand lane
d make a U-turn at the next gap in the central reservation

## Question 9.39 NI Exempt

Mark one answer

Your vehicle breaks down on the hard shoulder of a motorway. You decide to use your mobile phone to call for help. You should

a  stand at the rear of the vehicle while making the call
b  try to repair the vehicle yourself
c  get out of the vehicle by the right-hand door
d  check your location from the marker posts on the left

## Question 9.40

Mark one answer

You are driving a car on a motorway. Unless signs show otherwise you must NOT exceed

a  50mph
b  60mph
c  70mph
d  80mph

## Question 9.41 NI Exempt

Mark one answer

You are on a three-lane motorway towing a trailer. You may use the right-hand lane when

a  there are lane closures
b  there is slow-moving traffic
c  you can maintain a high speed
d  large vehicles are in the left and centre lanes

## Question 9.42

Mark one answer

You are on a motorway. There is a contraflow system ahead. What would you expect to find?

a  Temporary traffic lights
b  Lower speed limits
c  Wider lanes than normal
d  Speed humps

## Question 9.43

Mark one answer

You are driving at 70mph on a three-lane motorway. There is no traffic ahead. Which lane should you use?

a  Any lane
b  Middle lane
c  Right lane
d  Left lane

## Question 9.44

Mark one answer
Your vehicle has broken down on a motorway. You are not able to stop on the hard shoulder. What should you do?

a Switch on your hazard warning lights
b Stop following traffic and ask for help
c Attempt to repair your vehicle quickly
d Stand behind your vehicle to warn others

## Question 9.45

Mark one answer
Why is it particularly important to carry out a check on your vehicle before making a long motorway journey?

a You will have to do more harsh braking on motorways
b Motorway service stations do not deal with breakdowns
c The road surface will wear down the tyres faster
d Continuous high speeds may increase the risk of your vehicle breaking down

## Question 9.46

Mark one answer
For what reason may you use the right-hand lane of a motorway?

a For keeping out of the way of lorries
b For driving at more than 70mph
c For turning right
d For overtaking other vehicles

## Question 9.47

Mark one answer
On a motorway you may only stop on the hard shoulder

a in an emergency
b if you feel tired and need to rest
c if you accidentally go past the exit that you wanted to take
d to pick up a hitchhiker

## Question 9.48

Mark one answer

You are driving on a motorway. The car ahead shows its hazard lights for a short time. This tells you that

a  the driver wants you to overtake
b  the other car is going to change lanes
c  traffic ahead is slowing or stopping suddenly
d  there is a police speed check ahead

## Question 9.49

Mark one answer

The emergency telephones on a motorway are connected to the

a  ambulance service
b  police control
c  fire brigade
d  breakdown service

## Question 9.50

Mark one answer

You are intending to leave the motorway at the next exit. Before you reach the exit you should normally position your vehicle

a  in the middle lane
b  in the left-hand lane
c  on the hard shoulder
d  in any lane

## Question 9.51

Mark one answer

As a provisional licence holder you should not drive a car

a  over 30mph
b  at night
c  on the motorway
d  with passengers in rear seats

## Answers and explanations

9.1    a, d, e, f

9.2    a, d, e, f

9.3    d

9.4    d

9.5    d

9.6    d Speed limits may be altered due to weather conditions. Look out for signs on the central reserve or above your lane.

9.7    a Strictly speaking, any vehicle which is allowed on a motorway.

9.8    b

9.9    c

9.10   b, e

9.11   c

9.12   a You may only stop on the hard shoulder in an emergency.

9.13   c

9.14   a

9.15   d

9.16   a

9.17   c

9.18   c

9.19   c

9.20   c

9.21   c

9.22   c

9.23   b

9.24   c You need to build up your speed to that of the traffic already on the motorway so you can ease into a gap in the flow of traffic.

9.25   b

9.26   b

9.27   a The other lanes should be used for overtaking.

9.28   b

9.29   b In these circumstances there may also be a speed limit – keep to it.

9.30   d

9.31   c, d, f
Service areas are not officially part of the motorway.

9.32   c In motorway roadworks you are sometimes, but not always, directed to use the hard shoulder, especially where the right-hand lane is closed. Therefore, 'b' is not correct. There often are lower speed limits to protect the traffic in contraflows or narrow lanes and you must obey these.

9.33   d You should note the variable speed limit areas of the M25, where it is permissible to overtake in the left lane and drivers are encouraged to stay in the lane they are travelling in.

9.34   c

9.35   d

9.36   a

9.37   b It is dangerous to attempt to change the wheel yourself. Try to keep as far from the carriageway as possible while waiting for assistance.

9.38   b

9.39   d

9.40   c

9.41   a

9.42   b

9.43   d You should always use the left-hand lane for normal driving.

9.44   a

9.45   <u>d</u> Check oil and windscreen
washer levels and also check
the tyres. Plan your rest stops.

9.46   <u>d</u>

9.47   <u>a</u>

9.48   <u>c</u>

9.49   <u>b</u>

9.50   <u>b</u>

9.51   <u>c</u>

# Theory Test Questions for Car Drivers

## 2004–2005

Section 10 Rules of the road

## Question 10.1

Mark one answer
What is the meaning of this sign?

a   Local speed limit applies
b   No waiting on the carriageway
c   National speed limit applies
d   No entry to vehicular traffic

## Question 10.2

Mark one answer
What is the national speed limit on a single carriageway road for cars and motorcycles?

a   70mph
b   60mph
c   50mph
d   30mph

## Question 10.3

Mark one answer
What is the national speed limit for cars and motorcycles on a dual carriageway?

a   30mph
b   50mph
c   60mph
d   70mph

## Question 10.4

Mark one answer
There are no speed limit signs on the road. How is a 30mph limit indicated?

a   By hazard warning lines
b   By street lighting
c   By pedestrian islands
d   By double or single yellow lines

## Question 10.5

Mark one answer
Where you see street lights but no speed limit signs the limit is usually

a   30mph
b   40mph
c   50mph
d   60mph

## Question 10.6

Mark one answer
What does this sign mean?

a   Minimum speed 30mph
b   End of maximum speed
c   End of minimum speed
d   Maximum speed 30mph

## Question 10.7

Mark one answer

There is a tractor ahead of you. You wish to overtake but you are NOT sure if it is safe to do so. You should

a   follow another overtaking vehicle through
b   sound your horn to the slow vehicle to pull over
c   speed through but flash your lights to oncoming traffic
d   not overtake if you are in doubt

## Question 10.8

Mark three answers

Which three of the following are most likely to take an unusual course at roundabouts?

a   Horse riders
b   Milk floats
c   Delivery vans
d   Long vehicles
e   Estate cars
f   Cyclists

## Question 10.9

Mark four answers

In which FOUR places must you NOT park or wait?

a   On a dual carriageway
b   At a bus stop
c   On the slope of a hill
d   Opposite a traffic island
e   In front of someone else's drive
f   On the brow of a hill

## Question 10.10

Mark two answers

In which TWO places must you NOT park?

a   Near a school entrance
b   Near a police station
c   In a side road
d   At a bus stop
e   In a one-way street

## Question 10.11

Mark one answer

On a clearway you must not stop

a   at any time
b   when it is busy
c   in the rush hour
d   during daylight hours

## Question 10.12

Mark one answer
What is the meaning of this sign?

a   No entry
b   Waiting restrictions
c   National speed limit
d   School crossing patrol

## Question 10.13

Mark one answer
You can park on the right-hand side of a road at night

a   in a one-way street
b   with your sidelights on
c   more than 10 metres (32 feet) from a junction
d   under a lamp-post

## Question 10.14

Mark one answer
On a three-lane dual carriageway the right-hand lane can be used for

a   overtaking only, never turning right
b   overtaking or turning right
c   fast-moving traffic only
d   turning right only, never overtaking

## Question 10.15

Mark one answer
You are approaching a busy junction. There are several lanes with road markings. At the last moment you realise that you are in the wrong lane. You should

a   continue in that lane
b   force your way across
c   stop until the area has cleared
d   use clear arm signals to cut across

## Question 10.16

Mark one answer
Where may you overtake on a one-way street?

a   Only on the left-hand side
b   Overtaking is not allowed
c   Only on the right-hand side
d   Either on the right or the left

## Question 10.17

Mark one answer
When going straight ahead at a roundabout you should

a   indicate left before leaving the roundabout
b   not indicate at any time
c   indicate right when approaching the roundabout
d   indicate left when approaching the roundabout

## Question 10.18

Mark one answer
Which vehicle might have to use a different course to normal at roundabouts?

a   Sports car
b   Van
c   Estate car
d   Long vehicle

## Question 10.19

Mark one answer
You are going straight ahead at a roundabout. How should you signal?

a   Signal right on the approach and then left to leave the roundabout
b   Signal left as you leave the roundabout
c   Signal left on the approach to the roundabout and keep the signal on until you leave
d   Signal left just after you pass the exit before the one you will take

## Question 10.20

Mark one answer
You may only enter a box junction when

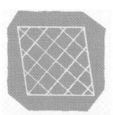

a   there are less than two vehicles in front of you
b   the traffic lights show green
c   your exit road is clear
d   you need to turn left

## Question 10.21

Mark one answer
You may wait in a yellow box junction when

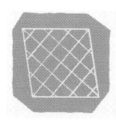

a   oncoming traffic is preventing you from turning right
b   you are in a queue of traffic turning left
c   you are in a queue of traffic to go ahead
d   you are on a roundabout

## Question 10.22

Mark three answers
You MUST stop when signalled to do so by which THREE of these?

a A police officer
b A pedestrian
c A school crossing patrol
d A bus driver
e A red traffic light

## Question 10.23

Mark one answer
You will see these markers when approaching

a the end of a motorway
b a concealed level crossing
c a concealed speed limit sign
d the end of a dual carriageway

## Question 10.24

Mark one answer
Someone is waiting to cross at a zebra crossing. They are standing on the pavement. You should normally

a go on quickly before they step onto the crossing
b stop before you reach the zigzag lines and let them cross
c stop, let them cross, wait patiently
d ignore them as they are still on the pavement

## Question 10.25

Mark one answer
At toucan crossings, apart from pedestrians you should be aware of

a emergency vehicles emerging
b buses pulling out
c trams crossing in front
d cyclists riding across

## Question 10.26

Mark two answers
Who can use a toucan crossing?

a Trains
b Cyclists
c Buses
d Pedestrians
e Trams

## Question 10.27

Mark one answer

At a pelican crossing, what does a flashing amber light mean?

a  You must not move off until the lights stop flashing
b  You must give way to pedestrians still on the crossing
c  You can move off, even if pedestrians are still on the crossing
d  You must stop because the lights are about to change to red

## Question 10.28

Mark one answer

You are waiting at a pelican crossing. The red light changes to flashing amber. This means you must

a  wait for pedestrians on the crossing to clear
b  move off immediately without any hesitation
c  wait for the green light before moving off
d  get ready and go when the continuous amber light shows

## Question 10.29

Mark one answer

You are travelling on a well-lit road at night in a built-up area. By using dipped headlights you will be able to

a  see further along the road
b  go at a much faster speed
c  switch to main beam quickly
d  be easily seen by others

## Question 10.30

Mark one answer

When can you park on the left opposite these road markings?

a  If the line nearest to you is broken
b  When there are no yellow lines
c  To pick up or set down passengers
d  During daylight hours only

## Question 10.31

Mark one answer
You are intending to turn right at a crossroads. An oncoming driver is also turning right. It will normally be safer to

a keep the other vehicle to your RIGHT and turn behind it (offside to offside)
b keep the other vehicle to your LEFT and turn in front of it (nearside to nearside)
c carry on and turn at the next junction instead
d hold back and wait for the other driver to turn first

## Question 10.32

Mark one answer
You are on a road that has no traffic signs. There are street lights. What is the speed limit?

a 20mph
b 30mph
c 40mph
d 60mph

## Question 10.33

Mark three answers
You are going along a street with parked vehicles on the left-hand side. For which THREE reasons should you keep your speed down?

a So that oncoming traffic can see you more clearly
b You may set off car alarms
c Vehicles may be pulling out
d Drivers' doors may open
e Children may run out from between the vehicles

## Question 10.34

Mark one answer
You meet an obstruction on your side of the road. You should

a carry on, you have priority
b give way to oncoming traffic
c wave oncoming vehicles through
d accelerate to get past first

## Question 10.35

Mark two answers

You are on a two-lane dual carriageway. For which TWO of the following would you use the right-hand lane?

a  Turning right
b  Normal progress
c  Staying at the minimum allowed speed
d  Constant high speed
e  Overtaking slower traffic
f  Mending punctures

## Question 10.36

Mark one answer

Who has priority at an unmarked crossroads?

a  The larger vehicle
b  No one has priority
c  The faster vehicle
d  The smaller vehicle

## Question 10.37 NI Exempt

Mark one answer

What is the nearest you may park to a junction?

a  10 metres (32 feet)
b  12 metres (39 feet)
c  15 metres (49 feet)
d  20 metres (66 feet)

## Question 10.38 NI Exempt

Mark three answers

In which THREE places must you NOT park?

a  Near the brow of a hill
b  At or near a bus stop
c  Where there is no pavement
d  Within 10 metres (32 feet) of a junction
e  On a 40mph road

## Question 10.39

Mark one answer

You are waiting at a level crossing. A train has passed but the lights keep flashing. You must

a  carry on waiting
b  phone the signal operator
c  edge over the stop line and look for trains
d  park and investigate

## Question 10.40

Mark one answer

You park overnight on a road with a 40mph speed limit. You should park

a  facing the traffic
b  with parking lights on
c  with dipped headlights on
d  near a street light

## Question 10.41

Mark one answer
The dual carriageway you are turning right onto has a very narrow central reserve. What should you do?

a  Proceed to the central reserve and wait
b  Wait until the road is clear in both directions
c  Stop in the first lane so that other vehicles give way
d  Emerge slightly to show your intentions

## Question 10.42

Mark one answer
What does this sign tell you?

a  That it is a no-through road
b  End of traffic calming zone
c  Free parking zone ends
d  No waiting zone ends

## Question 10.43

Mark one answer
At a crossroads there are no signs or road markings. Two vehicles approach. Which has priority?

a  Neither of the vehicles
b  The vehicle travelling the fastest
c  Oncoming vehicles turning right
d  Vehicles approaching from the right

## Question 10.44

Mark one answer
You are entering an area of roadworks. There is a temporary speed limit displayed. You should

a  not exceed the speed limit
b  obey the limit only during rush hour
c  ignore the displayed limit
d  obey the limit except at night

## Question 10.45

Mark one answer
You may drive over a footpath

a  to overtake slow-moving traffic
b  when the pavement is very wide
c  if no pedestrians are near
d  to get into a property

## Question 10.46

Mark one answer
A single carriageway road has this sign. What is the maximum permitted speed for a car towing a trailer?

a  30mph
b  40mph
c  50mph
d  60mph

## Question 10.47

Mark one answer
You are towing a small caravan on a dual carriageway. You must not exceed

a  50mph
b  40mph
c  70mph
d  60mph

## Question 10.48

Mark one answer
You want to park and you see this sign. On the days and times shown you should

**Meter ZONE**

**Mon - Fri**
**8.30 am - 6.30 pm**
**Saturday**
**8.30 am - 1.30 pm**

a  park in a bay and not pay
b  park on yellow lines and pay
c  park on yellow lines and not pay
d  park in a bay and pay

## Question 10.49

Mark three answers
As a car driver which THREE lanes are you NOT normally allowed to use?

a  Crawler lane
b  Bus lane
c  Overtaking lane
d  Acceleration lane
e  Cycle lane
f  Tram lane

## Question 10.50

Mark one answer
You are driving along a road that has a cycle lane. The lane is marked by a solid white line. This means that during its period of operation

a the lane may be used for parking your car
b you may drive in that lane at any time
c the lane may be used when necessary
d you must not drive in that lane

## Question 10.51

Mark one answer
A cycle lane is marked by a solid white line. You must not drive or park in it

a at any time
b during the rush hour
c if a cyclist is using it
d during its period of operation

## Question 10.52

Mark one answer
While driving, you intend to turn left into a minor road. On the approach you should

a keep just left of the middle of the road
b keep in the middle of the road
c swing out wide just before turning
d keep well to the left of the road

## Question 10.53

Mark one answer
You are waiting at a level crossing. The red warning lights continue to flash after a train has passed by. What should you do?

a Get out and investigate
b Telephone the signal operator
c Continue to wait
d Drive across carefully

## Question 10.54

Mark one answer
You are driving over a level crossing. The warning lights come on and a bell rings. What should you do?

a Get everyone out of the vehicle immediately
b Stop and reverse back to clear the crossing
c Keep going and clear the crossing
d Stop immediately and use your hazard warning lights

## Question 10.55

Mark one answer
You are on a busy main road and find that you are travelling in the wrong direction. What should you do?

a   Turn into a side road on the right and reverse into the main road
b   Make a U-turn in the main road
c   Make a 'three-point' turn in the main road
d   Turn round in a side road

## Question 10.56

Mark one answer
You may remove your seat belt when carrying out a manoeuvre that involves

a   reversing
b   a hill start
c   an emergency stop
d   driving slowly

## Question 10.57

Mark one answer
You must not reverse

a   for longer than necessary
b   for more than a car's length
c   into a side road
d   in a built-up area

## Question 10.58

Mark one answer
You are parked in a busy high street. What is the safest way to turn your vehicle around to go the opposite way?

a   Find a quiet side road to turn round in
b   Drive into a side road and reverse into the main road
c   Get someone to stop the traffic
d   Do a U-turn

## Question 10.59

Mark one answer
When you are NOT sure that it is safe to reverse your vehicle you should

a   use your horn
b   rev your engine
c   get out and check
d   reverse slowly

## Question 10.60

Mark one answer
When may you reverse from a side road into a main road?

a   Only if both roads are clear of traffic
b   Not at any time
c   At any time
d   Only if the main road is clear of traffic

167

## Question 10.61

Mark one answer
You want to turn right at a box junction. There is oncoming traffic. You should

a wait in the box junction if your exit is clear
b wait before the junction until it is clear of all traffic
c drive on, you cannot turn right at a box junction
d drive slowly into the box junction when signalled by oncoming traffic

## Question 10.62

Mark one answer
You are reversing your vehicle into a side road. When would the greatest hazard to passing traffic occur?

a After you've completed the manoeuvre
b Just before you actually begin to manoeuvre
c After you've entered the side road
d When the front of your vehicle swings out

## Question 10.63

Mark two answers
You are driving on a road that has a cycle lane. The lane is marked by a broken white line. This means that

a you should not drive in the lane unless it is unavoidable
b you should not park in the lane unless it is unavoidable
c you can drive in the lane at any time
d the lane must be used by motorcyclists in heavy traffic

## Question 10.64

Mark one answer
Where is the safest place to park your vehicle at night?

a In a garage
b On a busy road
c In a quiet car park
d Near a red route

## Question 10.65

Mark one answer
To help keep your vehicle secure at night where should you park?

a Near a police station
b In a quiet road
c On a red route
d In a well-lit area

## Question 10.66

Mark one answer
You are in the right-hand lane of a dual carriageway. You see signs showing that the right lane is closed 800 yards ahead. You should

a   keep in that lane until you reach the queue
b   move to the left immediately
c   wait and see which lane is moving faster
d   move to the left in good time

## Question 10.67

Mark one answer
You are driving on an urban clearway. You may stop only to

a   set down and pick up passengers
b   use a mobile telephone
c   ask for directions
d   load or unload goods

## Question 10.68

Mark one answer
You are looking for somewhere to park your vehicle. The area is full EXCEPT for spaces marked 'disabled use'. You can

a   use these spaces when elsewhere is full
b   park if you stay with your vehicle
c   use these spaces, disabled or not
d   not park there unless permitted

## Question 10.69

Mark one answer
Your vehicle is parked on the road at night. When must you use sidelights?

a   Where there are continuous white lines in the middle of the road
b   Where the speed limit exceeds 30mph
c   Where you are facing oncoming traffic
d   Where you are near a bus stop

## Question 10.70

Mark three answers
On which THREE occasions MUST you stop your vehicle?

a   When involved in an accident
b   At a red traffic light
c   When signalled to do so by a police officer
d   At a junction with double broken white lines
e   At a pelican crossing when the amber light is flashing and no pedestrians are crossing

## Question 10.71

Mark one answer
You are on a road that is only wide enough for one vehicle. There is a car coming towards you. What should you do?

a   Pull into a passing place on your right
b   Force the other driver to reverse
c   Pull into a passing place if your vehicle is wider
d   Pull into a passing place on your left

## Question 10.72

Mark one answer
What MUST you have to park in a disabled space?

a   An orange or blue badge
b   A wheelchair
c   An advanced driver certificate
d   A modified vehicle

## Question 10.73

Mark one answer
You are driving at night with full beam headlights on. A vehicle is overtaking you. You should dip your lights

a   some time after the vehicle has passed you
b   before the vehicle starts to pass you
c   only if the other driver dips their headlights
d   as soon as the vehicle passes you

## Question 10.74

Mark one answer

When may you drive a motor car in this bus lane?

a   Outside its hours of operation
b   To get to the front of a traffic queue
c   You may not use it at any time
d   To overtake slow-moving traffic

## Question 10.75

Mark one answer

Signals are normally given by direction indicators and

a   brake lights
b   side lights
c   fog lights
d   interior lights

## Answers and explanations

10.1   c
10.2   b
10.3   d The national speed limit is 70mph on a motorway or dual carriageway and 60mph on two-way roads unless traffic signs denote anything different.
10.4   b
10.5   a
10.6   c
10.7   d
10.8   a, d, f
10.9   b, d, e, f
10.10  a, d
10.11  a
10.12  b
10.13  a
10.14  b
10.15  a All the other actions suggested could be dangerous.
10.16  d
10.17  a You should signal left just as you pass the exit before the one you want to take.
10.18  d
10.19  d
10.20  c
10.21  a
10.22  a, c, e
       Note the word 'MUST' in the question, which is asking what the law says.
10.23  b These countdown markers indicate the distance to the stop line at the concealed level crossing.
10.24  c

10.25 d Cyclists are allowed to ride across toucan crossings, unlike other crossings where they must dismount.

10.26 b, d
Toucan crossings are shared by pedestrians and cyclists together.

10.27 b You may drive as soon as the crossing is clear and before the flashing amber light changes to green.

10.28 a

10.29 d

10.30 c

10.31 a This is because passing offside-to-offside your view will not be blocked by the oncoming car that also wishes to turn right.

10.32 b If there are street lights, the speed limit is 30mph unless a road sign states otherwise.

10.33 c, d, e

10.34 b

10.35 a, e

10.36 b An unmarked crossroads has no road signs or road markings and no vehicle has priority even if one road is wider or busier than the other.

10.37 a

10.38 a, b, d

10.39 a

10.40 b

10.41 b Because the central reserve is narrow, you would partly block the road if you drove to the middle and had to wait.

10.42 d

10.43 a You often find these on housing estates. Approach with caution and be prepared to give way.

10.44 a

10.45 d

10.46 c

10.47 d

10.48 d

10.49 b, e, f

10.50 d

10.51 d

10.52 d

10.53 c You should wait for three minutes. If no further train passes you should telephone the signal operator.

10.54 c You are already on the crossing when the warning lights come on, so 'c' is correct.

10.55 d It is illegal to reverse from a minor to a major road, so 'a' is wrong. 'b' and 'c' would be dangerous because the road is busy.

10.56 a

10.57 a

10.58 a

10.59 c

10.60 b

10.61 a

10.62 d Always remember to check all round just before steering and give way to any road users.

10.63 a, b

10.64 a

10.65 d

10.66 d

10.67 a

10.68 d

10.69 b

10.70 a, b, c
'd' is wrong because although the double, broken white lines at a junction mean 'give way', you do not necessarily have to stop in order to do so. 'e' is wrong because you may drive on at a pelican crossing when the amber light is flashing if no pedestrians are crossing.

10.71 d

10.72 a Since April 1, 2000 the Orange Badge scheme has been known as the Blue Badge scheme.

10.73 d If you dip your lights too early you may reduce your vision; too late and you may dazzle the driver who has overtaken.

10.74 a

10.75 a

# Theory Test Questions for Car Drivers

2004–2005

Section 11    Road and
traffic signs

## Question 11.1

Mark one answer
You MUST obey signs giving orders.
These signs are mostly in

a   green rectangles
b   red triangles
c   blue rectangles
d   red circles

## Question 11.2

Mark one answer
Traffic signs giving orders are generally which shape?

a        b        c        d

## Question 11.3

Mark one answer
Which type of sign tells you NOT to do something?

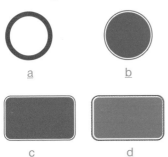

## Question 11.4

Mark one answer
What does this sign mean?

a   Maximum speed limit with traffic calming
b   Minimum speed limit with traffic calming
c   '20 cars only' parking zone
d   Only 20 cars allowed at any one time

## Question 11.5

Mark one answer
Which sign means no motor vehicles are allowed?

176

## Question 11.6

Mark one answer
Which of these signs means no motor vehicles?

a

b

c

d

## Question 11.7

Mark one answer
What does this sign mean?

a   New speed limit 20mph
b   No vehicles over 30 tonnes
c   Minimum speed limit 30mph
d   End of 20mph zone

## Question 11.8

Mark one answer
What does this sign mean?

a   No overtaking
b   No motor vehicles
c   Clearway (no stopping)
d   Cars and motorcycles only

## Question 11.9

Mark one answer
What does this sign mean?

a   No parking
b   No road markings
c   No through road
d   No entry

## Question 11.10

Mark one answer
What does this sign mean?

a  Bend to the right
b  Road on the right closed
c  No traffic from the right
d  No right turn

## Question 11.11

Mark one answer
Which sign means 'no entry'?

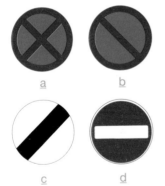

a               b

c               d

## Question 11.12

Mark one answer
What does this sign mean?

a  Route for trams only
b  Route for buses only
c  Parking for buses only
d  Parking for trams only

## Question 11.13

Mark one answer
Which type of vehicle does this sign apply to?

a  Wide vehicles
b  Long vehicles
c  High vehicles
d  Heavy vehicles

## Question 11.14

Mark one answer
Which sign means NO motor vehicles allowed?

a

b

c

d

## Question 11.15

Mark one answer
What does this sign mean?

a    You have priority
b    No motor vehicles
c    Two-way traffic
d    No overtaking

## Question 11.16

Mark one answer
What does this sign mean?

a    Keep in one lane
b    Give way to oncoming traffic
c    Do not overtake
d    Form two lanes

## Question 11.17

Mark one answer
Which sign means no overtaking?

a

b

c

d

## Question 11.18

Mark one answer
What does this sign mean?

a   Waiting restrictions apply
b   Waiting permitted
c   National speed limit applies
d   Clearway (no stopping)

## Question 11.19

Mark one answer
What does this sign mean?

a   End of restricted speed area
b   End of restricted parking area
c   End of clearway
d   End of cycle route

## Question 11.20

Mark one answer
Which sign means 'no stopping'?

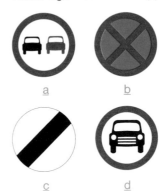

a                          b

c                          d

## Question 11.21

Mark one answer
What does this sign mean?

a   Roundabout
b   Crossroads
c   No stopping
d   No entry

## Question 11.22

Mark one answer
You see this sign ahead. It means

a   national speed limit applies
b   waiting restrictions apply
c   no stopping
d   no entry

## Question 11.23

Mark one answer
What does this sign mean?

a   Distance to parking place ahead
b   Distance to public telephone ahead
c   Distance to public house ahead
d   Distance to passing place ahead

## Question 11.24

Mark one answer
What does this sign mean?

a   Vehicles may not park on the verge or footway
b   Vehicles may park on the left-hand side of the road only
c   Vehicles may park fully on the verge or footway
d   Vehicles may park on the right-hand side of the road only

## Question 11.25

Mark one answer
What does this traffic sign mean?

a   No overtaking allowed
b   Give priority to oncoming traffic
c   Two-way traffic
d   One-way traffic only

## Question 11.26

Mark one answer
What is the meaning of this traffic sign?

a  End of two-way road
b  Give priority to vehicles coming towards you
c  You have priority over vehicles coming towards you
d  Bus lane ahead

## Question 11.27

Mark one answer
What MUST you do when you see this sign?

a  Stop, ONLY if traffic is approaching
b  Stop, even if the road is clear
c  Stop, ONLY if children are waiting to cross
d  Stop, ONLY if a red light is showing

## Question 11.28

Mark one answer
What does this sign mean?

a  No overtaking
b  You are entering a one-way street
c  Two-way traffic ahead
d  You have priority over vehicles from the opposite direction

## Question 11.29

Mark one answer
What shape is a STOP sign at a junction?

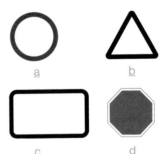

a          b

c          d

## Question 11.30

Mark one answer

At a junction you see this sign partly covered by snow. What does it mean?

a   Crossroads
b   Give way
c   Stop
d   Turn right

## Question 11.31

Mark one answer

Which shape is used for a GIVE WAY sign?

a   b

c   d

## Question 11.32

Mark one answer

What does this sign mean?

a   Service area 30 miles ahead
b   Maximum speed 30mph
c   Minimum speed 30mph
d   Lay-by 30 miles ahead

## Question 11.33

Mark one answer

Which of these signs means turn left ahead?

a   b

c   d

## Question 11.34

Mark one answer
What does this sign mean?

a Buses turning
b Ring road
c Mini roundabout
d Keep right

## Question 11.35

Mark one answer
What does this sign mean?

a Give way to oncoming vehicles
b Approaching traffic passes you on both sides
c Turn off at the next available junction
d Pass either side to get to the same destination

## Question 11.36

Mark one answer
What does this sign mean?

a Route for trams
b Give way to trams
c Route for buses
d Give way to buses

## Question 11.37

Mark one answer
What does a circular traffic sign with a blue background do?

a Give warning of a motorway ahead
b Give directions to a car park
c Give motorway information
d Give an instruction

## Question 11.38

Mark one answer
Which of these signs means that you are entering a one-way street?

a

b

c

d

## Question 11.39

Mark one answer
Where would you see a contraflow bus and cycle lane?

a  On a dual carriageway
b  On a roundabout
c  On an urban motorway
d  On a one-way street

## Question 11.40

Mark one answer
What does this sign mean?

a  Bus station on the right
b  Contraflow bus lane
c  With-flow bus lane
d  Give way to buses

## Question 11.41

Mark one answer
What does this sign mean?

a  With-flow bus and cycle lane
b  Contraflow bus and cycle lane
c  No buses and cycles allowed
d  No waiting for buses and cycles

## Question 11.42

Mark one answer
What does a sign with a brown background show?

a  Tourist directions
b  Primary roads
c  Motorway routes
d  Minor routes

## Question 11.43

Mark one answer
This sign means

a  tourist attraction
b  beware of trains
c  level crossing
d  beware of trams

## Question 11.44

Mark one answer
What are triangular signs for?

a  To give warnings
b  To give information
c  To give orders
d  To give directions

## Question 11.45

Mark one answer
What does this sign mean?

a  Turn left ahead
b  T-junction
c  No through road
d  Give way

## Question 11.46

Mark one answer

What does this sign mean?

a  Multi-exit roundabout
b  Risk of ice
c  Six roads converge
d  Place of historical interest

## Question 11.47

Mark one answer

What does this sign mean?

a  Crossroads
b  Level crossing with gate
c  Level crossing without gate
d  Ahead only

## Question 11.48

Mark one answer

What does this sign mean?

a  Ring road
b  Mini-roundabout
c  No vehicles
d  Roundabout

## Question 11.49

Mark four answers

Which FOUR of these would be indicated by a triangular road sign?

a  Road narrows
b  Ahead only
c  Low bridge
d  Minimum speed
e  Children crossing
f  T-junction

## Question 11.50

Mark one answer
What does this sign mean?

a  Cyclists must dismount
b  Cycles are not allowed
c  Cycle route ahead
d  Cycle in single file

## Question 11.51

Mark one answer
Which sign means that pedestrians may be walking along the road?

a

b

c

d

## Question 11.52

Mark one answer
Which of these signs warn you of a pedestrian crossing?

a

b

c

d

## Question 11.53

Mark one answer
What does this sign mean?

a  No footpath ahead
b  Pedestrians only ahead
c  Pedestrian crossing ahead
d  School crossing ahead

## Question 11.54

Mark one answer

What does this sign mean?

a   School crossing patrol
b   No pedestrians allowed
c   Pedestrian zone – no vehicles
d   Pedestrian crossing ahead

## Question 11.55

Mark one answer

Which of these signs means there is a double bend ahead?

## Question 11.56

Mark one answer

What does this sign mean?

a   Wait at the barriers
b   Wait at the crossroads
c   Give way to trams
d   Give way to farm vehicles

## Question 11.57

Mark one answer

What does this sign mean?

a   Humpback bridge
b   Humps in the road
c   Entrance to tunnel
d   Soft verges

## Question 11.58

<u>Mark one answer</u>
What does this sign mean?

a  Low bridge ahead
b  Tunnel ahead
c  Ancient monument ahead
d  Accident black spot ahead

## Question 11.59

<u>Mark one answer</u>
What does this sign mean?

a  Two-way traffic straight ahead
b  Two-way traffic crossing a one-way street
c  Two-way traffic over a bridge
d  Two-way traffic crosses a two-way road

## Question 11.60

<u>Mark one answer</u>
Which sign means 'two-way traffic crosses a one-way road'?

a                b

c                d

## Question 11.61

<u>Mark one answer</u>
Which of these signs means the end of a dual carriageway?

a                b

c                d

## Question 11.62

Mark one answer
What does this sign mean?

a  End of dual carriageway
b  Tall bridge
c  Road narrows
d  End of narrow bridge

## Question 11.63

Mark one answer
What does this sign mean?

a  Two-way traffic ahead across a one-way street
b  Traffic approaching you has priority
c  Two-way traffic straight ahead
d  Motorway contraflow system ahead

## Question 11.64

Mark one answer
What does this sign mean?

a  Crosswinds
b  Road noise
c  Airport
d  Adverse camber

## Question 11.65

Mark one answer
What does this traffic sign mean?

a  Slippery road ahead
b  Tyres liable to punctures ahead
c  Danger ahead
d  Service area ahead

## Question 11.66

Mark one answer
You are about to overtake when you see this sign. You should

a   overtake the other driver as quickly as possible
b   move to the right to get a better view
c   switch your headlights on before overtaking
d   hold back until you can see clearly ahead

## Question 11.67

Mark one answer
What does this sign mean?

a   Level crossing with gate or barrier
b   Gated road ahead
c   Level crossing without gate or barrier
d   Cattle grid ahead

## Question 11.68

Mark one answer
What does this sign mean?

a   No trams ahead
b   Oncoming trams
c   Trams crossing ahead
d   Trams only

## Question 11.69

Mark one answer
What does this sign mean?

a   Adverse camber
b   Steep hill downwards
c   Uneven road
d   Steep hill upwards

## Question 11.70

Mark one answer
What does this sign mean?

a  Uneven road surface
b  Bridge over the road
c  Road ahead ends
d  Water across the road

## Question 11.71

Mark one answer
What does this sign mean?

a  Humpback bridge
b  Traffic calming hump
c  Low bridge
d  Uneven road

## Question 11.72

Mark one answer
What does this sign mean?

a  Turn left for parking area
b  No through road on the left
c  No entry for traffic turning left
d  Turn left for ferry terminal

## Question 11.73

Mark one answer
What does this sign mean?

a  T-junction
b  No through road
c  Telephone box ahead
d  Toilet ahead

## Question 11.74

Mark one answer
Which sign means 'no through road'?

a

b

c

d

## Question 11.75

Mark one answer
Which of the following signs informs you that you are coming to a No Through Road?

a

b

c

d

## Question 11.76

Mark one answer
What does this sign mean?

a   Direction to park and ride car park
b   No parking for buses or coaches
c   Directions to bus and coach park
d   Parking area for cars and coaches

## Question 11.77

Mark one answer
You are driving through a tunnel and you see this sign. What does it mean?

a   Direction to emergency pedestrian exit
b   Beware of pedestrians, no footpath ahead
c   No access for pedestrians
d   Beware of pedestrians crossing ahead

## Question 11.78

Mark one answer
Which is the sign for a ring road?

a

b

c

d

## Question 11.79

Mark one answer
What does this sign mean?

a  Route for lorries
b  Ring road
c  Rest area
d  Roundabout

## Question 11.80

Mark one answer
What does this sign mean?

a  Hilly road
b  Humps in road
c  Holiday route
d  Hospital route

## Question 11.81

Mark one answer
What does this sign mean?

a  The right-hand lane ahead is narrow
b  Right-hand lane for buses only
c  Right-hand lane for turning right
d  The right-hand lane is closed

195

## Question 11.82

Mark one answer
What does this sign mean?

a Change to the left lane
b Leave at the next exit
c Contraflow system
d One-way street

## Question 11.84

Mark one answer
What does this sign mean?

a Leave motorway at next exit
b Lane for heavy and slow vehicles
c All lorries use the hard shoulder
d Rest area for lorries

## Question 11.83

Mark three answers
To avoid an accident when entering a contraflow system, you should

a reduce speed in good time
b switch lanes anytime to make progress
c choose an appropriate lane early
d keep the correct separation distance
e increase speed to pass through quickly
f follow other motorists closely to avoid long queues

## Question 11.85

Mark one answer
You are approaching a red traffic light. The signal will change from red to

a red and amber, then green
b green, then amber
c amber, then green
d green and amber, then green

## Question 11.86

Mark one answer
A red traffic light means

a  you should stop unless turning left
b  stop, if you are able to brake safely
c  you must stop and wait behind the stop line
d  proceed with caution

## Question 11.87

Mark one answer
At traffic lights, amber on its own means

a  prepare to go
b  go if the way is clear
c  go if no pedestrians are crossing
d  stop at the stop line

## Question 11.88

Mark one answer
You are approaching traffic lights. Red and amber are showing. This means

a  pass the lights if the road is clear
b  there is a fault with the lights – take care
c  wait for the green light before you pass the lights
d  the lights are about to change to red

## Question 11.89

Mark one answer
You are at a junction controlled by traffic lights. When should you NOT proceed at green?

a  When pedestrians are waiting to cross
b  When your exit from the junction is blocked
c  When you think the lights may be about to change
d  When you intend to turn right

## Question 11.90

Mark one answer

You are in the left-hand lane at traffic lights. You are waiting to turn left. At which of these traffic lights must you NOT move on?

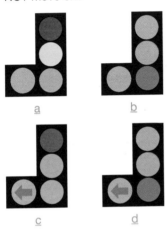

a      b

c      d

## Question 11.91

Mark one answer

What does this sign mean?

a   Traffic lights out of order
b   Amber signal out of order
c   Temporary traffic lights ahead
d   New traffic lights ahead

## Question 11.92

Mark one answer

When traffic lights are out of order, who has priority?

a   Traffic going straight on
b   Traffic turning right
c   Nobody
d   Traffic turning left

## Question 11.93

Mark three answers

These flashing red lights mean STOP. In which THREE of the following places could you find them?

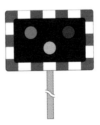

a   Pelican crossings
b   Lifting bridges
c   Zebra crossings
d   Level crossings
e   Motorway exits
f   Fire stations

## Question 11.94

Mark one answer
What do these zigzag lines at pedestrian crossings mean?

a   No parking at any time
b   Parking allowed only for a short time
c   Slow down to 20mph
d   Sounding horns is not allowed

## Question 11.95

Mark one answer
When may you cross a double solid white line in the middle of the road?

a   To pass traffic that is queuing back at a junction
b   To pass a car signalling to turn left ahead
c   To pass a road maintenance vehicle travelling at 10mph or less
d   To pass a vehicle that is towing a trailer

## Question 11.96

Mark one answer
What does this road marking mean?

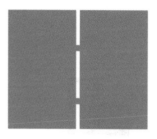

a   Do not cross the line
b   No stopping allowed
c   You are approaching a hazard
d   No overtaking allowed

## Question 11.97

Mark one answer
This marking appears on the road just before a

a   no entry sign
b   give way sign
c   stop sign
d   no through road sign

## Question 11.98

Mark one answer
Where would you see this road marking?

a At traffic lights
b On road humps
c Near a level crossing
d At a box junction

## Question 11.99

Mark one answer
Which is a hazard warning line?

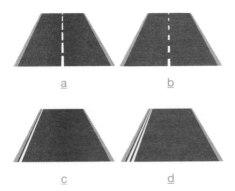

## Question 11.100

Mark one answer
At this junction there is a stop sign with a solid white line on the road surface. Why is there a stop sign here?

a Speed on the major road is de-restricted
b It is a busy junction
c Visibility along the major road is restricted
d There are hazard warning lines in the centre of the road

## Question 11.101

Mark one answer
You see this line across the road at the entrance to a roundabout. What does it mean?

a Give way to traffic from the right
b Traffic from the left has right of way
c You have right of way
d Stop at the line

## Question 11.102

Mark one answer
Where would you find this road marking?

a   At a railway crossing
b   At a junction
c   On a motorway
d   On a pedestrian crossing

## Question 11.103

Mark one answer
How will a police officer in a patrol vehicle normally get you to stop?

a   Flash the headlights, indicate left and point to the left
b   Wait until you stop, then approach you
c   Use the siren, overtake, cut in front and stop
d   Pull alongside you, use the siren and wave you to stop

## Question 11.104

Mark one answer
There is a police car following you. The police officer flashes the headlights and points to the left. What should you do?

a   Turn at the next left
b   Pull up on the left
c   Stop immediately
d   Move over to the left

## Question 11.105

Mark one answer
You approach a junction. The traffic lights are not working. A police officer gives this signal. You should

a   turn left only
b   turn right only
c   stop level with the officer's arm
d   stop at the stop line

## Question 11.106

Mark one answer
The driver of the car in front is giving this arm signal. What does it mean?

a   The driver is slowing down
b   The driver intends to turn right
c   The driver wishes to overtake
d   The driver intends to turn left

## Question 11.107

Mark one answer
Where would you see these road markings?

a   At a level crossing
b   On a motorway slip road
c   At a pedestrian crossing
d   On a single-track road

## Question 11.108

Mark one answer
When may you NOT overtake on the left?

a   On a free-flowing motorway or dual carriageway
b   When the traffic is moving slowly in queues
c   On a one-way street
d   When the car in front is signalling to turn right

## Question 11.109

Mark one answer
What does this motorway sign mean?

a   Change to the lane on your left
b   Leave the motorway at the next exit
c   Change to the opposite carriageway
d   Pull up on the hard shoulder

## Question 11.110

Mark one answer
What does this motorway sign mean?

a Temporary minimum speed 50mph
b No services for 50 miles
c Obstruction 50 metres (164 feet) ahead
d Temporary maximum speed 50mph

## Question 11.111

Mark one answer
What does this sign mean?

a Through traffic to use left lane
b Right-hand lane T-junction only
c Right-hand lane closed ahead
d 11 tonne weight limit

## Question 11.112

Mark one answer
On a motorway this sign means

a move over onto the hard shoulder
b overtaking on the left only
c leave the motorway at the next exit
d move to the lane on your left

## Question 11.113

Mark one answer
What does '25' mean on this motorway sign?

a The distance to the nearest town
b The route number of the road
c The number of the next junction
d The speed limit on the slip road

## Question 11.114

Mark one answer
The right-hand lane of a three-lane motorway is

a for lorries only
b an overtaking lane
c the right-turn lane
d an acceleration lane

## Question 11.115

Mark one answer
Where can you find reflective amber studs on a motorway?

a Separating the slip road from the motorway
b On the left-hand edge of the road
c On the right-hand edge of the road
d Separating the lanes

## Question 11.116

Mark one answer
Where on a motorway would you find green reflective studs?

a Separating driving lanes
b Between the hard shoulder and the carriageway
c At slip road entrances and exits
d Between the carriageway and the central reservation

## Question 11.117

Mark one answer
You are travelling along a motorway. You see this sign. You should

a leave the motorway at the next exit
b turn left immediately
c change lane
d move onto the hard shoulder

## Question 11.118

Mark one answer
What does this sign mean?

a No motor vehicles
b End of motorway
c No through road
d End of bus lane

## Question 11.119

Mark one answer
Which of these signs means that the national speed limit applies?

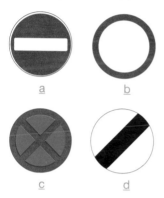

a          b

c          d

## Question 11.120

Mark one answer
What is the maximum speed on a single carriageway road?

a   50mph
b   60mph
c   40mph
d   70mph

## Question 11.121

Mark one answer
What does this sign mean?

a   End of motorway
b   End of restriction
c   Lane ends ahead
d   Free recovery ends

## Question 11.122

Mark one answer
This sign is advising you to

a   follow the route diversion
b   follow the signs to the picnic area
c   give way to pedestrians
d   give way to cyclists

## Question 11.123

Mark one answer
Why would this temporary speed limit
sign be shown?

a   To warn of the end of the motorway
b   To warn you of a low bridge
c   To warn you of a junction ahead
d   To warn of road works ahead

## Question 11.124

Mark one answer
This traffic sign means there is

a   a compulsory maximum speed limit
b   an advisory maximum speed limit
c   a compulsory minimum speed limit
d   an advised separation distance

## Question 11.125

Mark one answer
You see this sign at a crossroads.
You should

a   maintain the same speed
b   carry on with great care
c   find another route
d   telephone the police

## Question 11.126

Mark one answer
You are signalling to turn right in busy
traffic. How would you confirm your
intention safely?

a   Sound the horn
b   Give an arm signal
c   Flash your headlights
d   Position over the centre line

## Question 11.127

Mark one answer
What does this sign mean?

a   Motorcycles only
b   No cars
c   Cars only
d   No motorcycles

## Question 11.128

Mark one answer

You are on a motorway. You see this sign on a lorry that has stopped in the right-hand lane. You should

a  move into the right-hand lane
b  stop behind the flashing lights
c  pass the lorry on the left
d  leave the motorway at the next exit

## Question 11.129

Mark one answer

You are on a motorway. Red flashing lights appear above your lane only. What should you do?

a  Continue in that lane and look for further information
b  Move into another lane in good time
c  Pull onto the hard shoulder
d  Stop and wait for an instruction to proceed

## Question 11.130

Mark one answer

A red traffic light means

a  you must stop behind the white stop line
b  you may go straight on if there is no other traffic
c  you may turn left if it is safe to do so
d  you must slow down and prepare to stop if traffic has started to cross

## Question 11.131

Mark one answer

The driver of this car is giving an arm signal. What are they about to do?

a  Turn to the right
b  Turn to the left
c  Go straight ahead
d  Let pedestrians cross

## Question 11.132

Mark one answer
Which arm signal tells you that the car you are following is going to turn left?

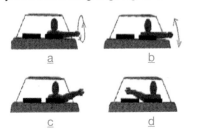

a     b

c     d

## Question 11.133

Mark one answer
When may you sound the horn?

a   To give you right of way
b   To attract a friend's attention
c   To warn others of your presence
d   To make slower drivers move over

## Question 11.134

Mark one answer
You must not use your horn when you are stationary

a   unless a moving vehicle may cause you danger
b   at any time whatsoever
c   unless it is used only briefly
d   except for signalling that you have just arrived

## Question 11.135

Mark one answer
What does this sign mean?

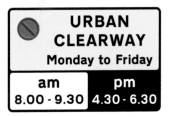

a   You can park on the days and times shown
b   No parking on the days and times shown
c   No parking at all from Monday to Friday
d   End of the urban clearway restrictions

## Question 11.136

Mark one answer
What does this sign mean?

a   Quayside or river bank
b   Steep hill downwards
c   Uneven road surface
d   Road liable to flooding

## Question 11.137

Mark one answer

You see this amber traffic light ahead.
Which light(s) will come on next?

  a  Red alone
  b  Red and amber together
  c  Green and amber together
  d  Green alone

## Question 11.138

Mark one answer

The white line painted in the centre of the road means

a  oncoming vehicles have priority over you
b  you should give priority to oncoming vehicles
c  there is a hazard ahead of you
d  the area is a national speed limit zone

## Question 11.139

Mark one answer

Which sign means you have priority over oncoming vehicles?

a

b

c

d

## Question 11.140

Mark one answer

You see this signal overhead on the motorway. What does it mean?

a  Leave the motorway at the next exit
b  All vehicles use the hard shoulder
c  Sharp bend to the left ahead
d  Stop all lanes ahead closed

## Question 11.141

Mark one answer

A white line like this along the centre of the road is a

a   bus lane marking
b   hazard warning
c   give way marking
d   lane marking

## Question 11.142

Mark one answer

What is the purpose of these yellow criss-cross lines on the road?

a   To make you more aware of the traffic lights
b   To guide you into position as you turn
c   To prevent the junction from becoming blocked
d   To show you where to stop when the lights change

## Question 11.143

Mark one answer

What is the reason for the yellow criss-cross lines painted on the road here?

a   To mark out an area for trams only
b   To prevent queuing traffic from blocking the junction on the left
c   To mark the entrance lane to a car park
d   To warn you of the tram lines crossing the road

## Question 11.144

Mark one answer

What is the reason for the area marked in red and white along the centre of this road?

a   It is to separate traffic flowing in opposite directions
b   It marks an area to be used by overtaking motorcyclists
c   It is a temporary marking to warn of the roadworks
d   It is separating the two sides of the dual carriageway

## Question 11.145

Mark one answer

Other drivers may sometimes flash their headlights at you. In which situation are they allowed to do this?

a   To warn of a radar speed trap ahead
b   To show that they are giving way to you
c   To warn you of their presence
d   To let you know there is a fault with your vehicle

## Question 11.146

Mark three answers

At road works which of the following can control traffic flow?

a   A STOP–GO board
b   Flashing amber lights
c   A police officer
d   Flashing red lights
e   Temporary traffic lights

## Question 11.147

Mark one answer

You are approaching a zebra crossing where pedestrians are waiting. Which arm signal might you give?

a                          b

c                          d

## Question 11.148

Mark one answer
Mark one answer
The white line along the side of the road

a  shows the edge of the carriageway
b  shows the approach to a hazard
c  means no parking
d  means no overtaking

## Question 11.149

Mark one answer
You see this white arrow on the road ahead. It means

a  entrance on the left
b  all vehicles turn left
c  keep left of the hatched markings
d  road bending to the left

## Question 11.150

Mark one answer
How should you give an arm signal to turn left?

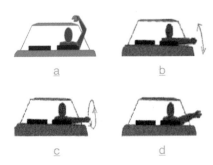

a               b

c               d

## Question 11.151

Mark one answer
You are waiting at a T-junction. A vehicle is coming from the right with the left signal flashing. What should you do?

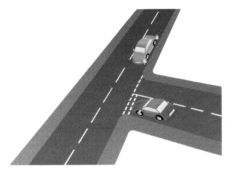

a  Move out and accelerate hard
b  Wait until the vehicle starts to turn in
c  Pull out before the vehicle reaches the junction
d  Move out slowly

## Question 11.152

Mark one answer
When may you use hazard warning lights when driving?

a   Instead of sounding the horn in a built-up area between 11.30 pm and 7 am
b   On a motorway or unrestricted dual carriageway, to warn of a hazard ahead
c   On rural routes, after a warning sign of animals
d   On the approach to toucan crossings where cyclists are waiting to cross

## Question 11.153

Mark one answer
You are driving on a motorway. There is a slow-moving vehicle ahead. On the back you see this sign. You should

a   pass on the right
b   pass on the left
c   leave at the next exit
d   drive no further

## Question 11.154

Mark one answer
You should NOT normally stop on these markings near schools

**⋀-SCHOOL KEEP CLEAR-⋀**

a   except when picking up children
b   under any circumstances
c   unless there is nowhere else available
d   except to set down children

## Question 11.155

Mark one answer
Why should you make sure that your indicators are cancelled after turning?

a   To avoid flattening the battery
b   To avoid misleading other road users
c   To avoid dazzling other road users
d   To avoid damage to the indicator relay

## Question 11.156

Mark one answer
You are driving in busy traffic. You want to pull up on the left just after a junction on the left. When should you signal?

a   As you are passing or just after the junction
b   Just before you reach the junction
c   Well before you reach the junction
d   It would be better not to signal at all

## Answers and explanations

11.1   d
11.2   d
11.3   a Red circles tell you what you must not do. Rectangles usually give you information.
11.4   a
11.5   b
11.6   a
11.7   d
11.8   b
11.9   d
11.10  d
11.11  d
11.12  a
11.13  c
11.14  b
11.15  d
11.16  c
11.17  b
11.18  a There will also be a plate indicating when the restriction applies.
11.19  b
11.20  b
11.21  c
11.22  c This is a clearway sign and you must not stop at all.
11.23  a
11.24  c
11.25  b
11.26  c
11.27  b You must always stop at a stop sign.
11.28  d
11.29  d

11.30  c The Stop sign is the only octagonal sign, allowing easy identification.
11.31  d The Give Way sign is the only triangular sign this way up, allowing easy recognition.
11.32  c
11.33  b
11.34  c
11.35  d
11.36  a
11.37  d Circular signs with blue backgrounds tell you what you must do.
11.38  b
11.39  d
11.40  b
11.41  a
11.42  a
11.43  a
11.44  a
11.45  b
11.46  b
11.47  a
11.48  d
11.49  a, c, e, f
11.50  c
11.51  a
11.52  a
11.53  c
11.54  d
11.55  b
11.56  c
11.57  b
11.58  b Red triangles usually give a warning.
11.59  b
11.60  b
11.61  d

| | |
|---|---|
| 11.62 | a |
| 11.63 | c |
| 11.64 | a |
| 11.65 | c |
| 11.66 | d It is dangerous to overtake when you see this sign because the dip in the road could be hiding oncoming traffic. |
| 11.67 | a |
| 11.68 | c |
| 11.69 | b |
| 11.70 | d |
| 11.71 | a |
| 11.72 | b |
| 11.73 | b |
| 11.74 | c |
| 11.75 | c |
| 11.76 | a |
| 11.77 | a |
| 11.78 | d |
| 11.79 | b |
| 11.80 | c |
| 11.81 | d |
| 11.82 | c |
| 11.83 | a, c, d |
| 11.84 | b |
| 11.85 | a The sequence of traffic lights is red, then red and amber, then green, then amber alone, then red. |
| 11.86 | c You must always stop at a red traffic light. |
| 11.87 | d An amber light means stop, and the lights will next change to red. |
| 11.88 | c The next light will be green and you must wait to drive on until it appears. |

| | |
|---|---|
| 11.89 | b |
| 11.90 | a |
| 11.91 | a |
| 11.92 | c |
| 11.93 | b, d, f |
| 11.94 | a |
| 11.95 | c |
| 11.96 | c |
| 11.97 | b |
| 11.98 | b |
| 11.99 | a Long lines with short gaps between them in the middle of the road are hazard warning lines. The more paint the more danger. |
| 11.100 | c Because the major road is on a bend, your vision is restricted to both left and right. |
| 11.101 | a |
| 11.102 | b |
| 11.103 | a |
| 11.104 | b You must stop, but 'c' is wrong because it may not be safe to stop immediately. |
| 11.105 | d |
| 11.106 | d |
| 11.107 | b |
| 11.108 | a You must not overtake on the left on a motorway or dual carriageway unless you are moving in queues of slow-moving traffic. |
| 11.109 | a Obviously you must make sure it is safe before doing so. |
| 11.110 | d |

11.111   c Always look well ahead and you will have plenty of time to react.

11.112   d You must go no further in that lane. You may change lanes and proceed, unless flashing red lights appear above all of them.

11.113   c

11.114   b

11.115   c

11.116   c

11.117   a

11.118   b

11.119   d

11.120   b

11.121   b

11.122   a

11.123   d

11.124   a

11.125   b

11.126   b

11.127   d

11.128   c

11.129   b

11.130   a

11.131   b

11.132   a

11.133   c Sounding your horn has the same meaning as flashing your headlights – to warn of your presence.

11.134   a

11.135   b

11.136   a

11.137   a

11.138   c

11.139   c

11.140   a

11.141   b

11.142   c

11.143   b

11.144   a

11.145   c 'c' is the correct answer because that is what flashing your headlights is supposed to mean. Not everyone knows or obeys the rules and they may flash their headlights for other reasons, so always try to make sure what they mean before you decide on any action.

11.146   a, c, e

11.147   a

11.148   a

11.149   c

11.150   c

11.151   b The approaching vehicle might have left the signal on by mistake, or intended to stop after the junction. Always wait long enough to be sure the vehicle is really turning left.

11.152   b Note that the question states 'when driving'. The types of roads in 'b' are the only places where it is legal to use hazard warning lights while your car is moving.

11.153   b

11.154   b

11.155   b

11.156   a

# Theory Test Questions for Car Drivers

## 2004–2005

## Section 12    Documents

## Question 12.1

<u>Mark one answer</u>
An MOT certificate is normally valid for

a   three years after the date it was issued
b   10,000 miles
c   one year after the date it was issued
d   30,000 miles

## Question 12.2

<u>Mark one answer</u>
A cover note is a document issued before you receive your

a   driving licence
b   insurance certificate
c   registration document
d   MOT certificate

## Question 12.3 NI Exempt

<u>Mark one answer</u>
A police officer asks to see your documents. You do not have them with you. You may produce them at a police station within

a   5 days
b   7 days
c   14 days
d   21 days

## Question 12.4

<u>Mark two answers</u>
You have just passed your practical test. You do not hold a full licence in another category. Within two years you get six penalty points on your licence. What will you have to do?

a   Retake only your theory test
b   Retake your theory and practical tests
c   Retake only your practical test
d   Reapply for your full licence immediately
e   Reapply for your provisional licence

## Question 12.5

<u>Mark one answer</u>
To drive on the road learners MUST

a   have NO penalty points on their licence
b   have taken professional instruction
c   have a signed, valid provisional licence
d   apply for a driving test within 12 months

## Question 12.6

Mark one answer

Before driving anyone else's motor vehicle you should make sure that

a   the vehicle owner has third party insurance cover
b   your own vehicle has insurance cover
c   the vehicle is insured for your use
d   the owner has left the insurance documents in the vehicle

## Question 12.7

Mark one answer

Your car needs an MOT certificate. If you drive without one this could invalidate your

a   vehicle service record
b   insurance
c   road tax disc
d   vehicle registration document

## Question 12.8

Mark two answers

To supervise a learner driver you must

a   have held a full licence for at least 3 years
b   be at least 21
c   be an approved driving instructor
d   hold an advanced driving certificate

## Question 12.9 NI Exempt

Mark one answer

When is it legal to drive a car over three years old without an MOT certificate?

a   Up to seven days after the old certificate has run out
b   When driving to an MOT centre to arrange an appointment
c   Just after buying a second-hand car with no MOT
d   When driving to an appointment at an MOT centre

## Question 12.10

Mark one answer

The cost of your insurance may be reduced if

a   your car is large and powerful
b   you are using the car for work purposes
c   you have penalty points on your licence
d   you are over 25 years old

## Question 12.11

Mark one answer

How old must you be to supervise a learner driver?

a   18 years old
b   19 years old
c   20 years old
d   21 years old

## Question 12.12

Mark one answer

A newly-qualified driver must

a   display green 'L' plates
b   not exceed 40mph for 12 months
c   be accompanied on a motorway
d   have valid motor insurance

## Question 12.13

Mark one answer

What is the legal minimum insurance cover you must have to drive on public roads?

a   Third party, fire and theft
b   Fully comprehensive
c   Third party only
d   Personal injury cover

## Question 12.14

Mark three answers

You have third party insurance. What does this cover?

a   Damage to your own vehicle
b   Damage to your vehicle by fire
c   Injury to another person
d   Damage to someone's property
e   Damage to other vehicles
f   Injury to yourself

## Question 12.15

Mark two answers

For which TWO of these must you show your motor insurance certificate?

a   When you are taking your driving test
b   When buying or selling a vehicle
c   When a police officer asks you for it
d   When you are taxing your vehicle
e   When having an MOT inspection

## Question 12.16

Mark one answer

Vehicle excise duty is often called 'Road Tax' or 'The Tax Disc'. You must

a   keep it with your registration document
b   display it clearly on your vehicle
c   keep it concealed safely in your vehicle
d   carry it on you at all times

## Question 12.17 NI Exempt

Mark one answer
Motor cars must FIRST have an MOT test certificate when they are

a   one year old
b   three years old
c   five years old
d   seven years old

## Question 12.18

Mark one answer
Your vehicle needs a current MOT certificate. You do not have one. Until you do have one you will not be able to renew your

a   driving licence
b   vehicle insurance
c   road tax disc
d   vehicle registration document

## Question 12.19

Mark three answers
Which THREE pieces of information are found on a vehicle registration document?

a   Registered keeper
b   Make of the vehicle
c   Service history details
d   Date of the MOT
e   Type of insurance cover
f   Engine size

## Question 12.20

Mark three answers
You have a duty to contact the licensing authority when

a   you go abroad on holiday
b   you change your vehicle
c   you change your name
d   your job status is changed
e   your permanent address changes
f   your job involves travelling abroad

## Question 12.21

Mark three answers
You must notify the licensing authority when

a   your health affects your driving
b   your eyesight does not meet a set standard
c   you intend lending your vehicle
d   your vehicle requires an MOT certificate
e   you change your vehicle

## Question 12.22

Mark one answer
You have just bought a secondhand vehicle. When should you tell the licensing authority of change of ownership?

a  Immediately
b  After 28 days
c  When an MOT is due
d  Only when you insure it

## Question 12.23

Mark two answers
Your vehicle is insured third party only. This covers

a  damage to your vehicle
b  damage to other vehicles
c  injury to yourself
d  injury to others
e  all damage and injury

## Question 12.24

Mark one answer
When you apply to renew your vehicle excise licence (tax disc) you must produce

a  a valid insurance certificate
b  the old tax disc
c  the vehicle handbook
d  a valid driving licence

## Question 12.25

Mark one answer
Your motor insurance policy has an excess of £100. What does this mean?

a  The insurance company will pay the first £100 of any claim
b  You will be paid £100 if you do not have an accident
c  Your vehicle is insured for a value of £100 if it is stolen
d  You will have to pay the first £100 of any claim

## Question 12.26

Mark one answer
What is the legal minimum insurance cover you must have to drive on public roads?

a  Fire and theft
b  Theft only
c  Third party
d  Fire only

## Question 12.27 NI Exempt

Mark one answer
The cost of your insurance may reduce if you

a  are under 25 years old
b  do not wear glasses
c  pass the driving test first time
d  take the Pass Plus scheme

## Question 12.28

<u>Mark three answers</u>
Which THREE of the following do you need before you can drive legally?

<u>a</u>  A valid driving licence with signature
<u>b</u>  A valid tax disc displayed on your vehicle
<u>c</u>  A vehicle service record
<u>d</u>  Proper insurance cover
<u>e</u>  Breakdown cover
<u>f</u>  A vehicle handbook

## Question 12.29 NI Exempt

<u>Mark one answer</u>
Which of the following may reduce the cost of your insurance?

<u>a</u>  Having a valid MOT certificate
<u>b</u>  Taking a Pass Plus course
<u>c</u>  Driving a powerful car
<u>d</u>  Having penalty points on your licence

## Question 12.30 NI Exempt

<u>Mark one answer</u>
The Pass Plus scheme has been created for new drivers. What is its main purpose?

<u>a</u>  To allow you to drive faster
<u>b</u>  To allow you to carry passengers
<u>c</u>  To improve your basic skills
<u>d</u>  To let you drive on motorways

## Answers and explanations

12.1  <u>c</u>
12.2  <u>b</u>
12.3  <u>b</u> You may select the police station of your choice.
12.4  <u>b, e</u>
12.5  <u>c</u> You are not allowed to drive until you have applied for and received your provisional licence and have signed it in ink.
12.6  <u>c</u> Your own vehicle insurance may cover you as a passenger in another person's vehicle but very rarely covers you to drive it.
12.7  <u>b</u>
12.8  <u>a, b</u>
12.9  <u>d</u> If your car is over three years old and has no valid MOT certificate, you must pre-book an appointment at an MOT centre before you drive it there.
12.10  <u>d</u> Drivers over 25 years old have less accidents than younger drivers. As they make fewer insurance claims, the cost of their premiums is usually less.
12.11  <u>d</u>
12.12  <u>d</u>
12.13  <u>c</u> This only covers damage to other people and their property.
12.14  <u>c, d, e</u>
12.15  <u>c, d</u>
12.16  <u>b</u>
12.17  <u>b</u>

12.18  c When you renew your road tax
disc you must produce a valid
certificate of insurance and also
a current MOT certificate if your
car is over three years old.

12.19  a, b, f

12.20  b, c, e

12.21  a, b, e

12.22  a

12.23  b, d

12.24  a

12.25  d Agreeing to pay an excess may
enable you to obtain a lower
premium.

12.26  c

12.27  d

12.28  a, b, d

12.29  b

12.30  c

# Theory Test Questions for Car Drivers

## 2004–2005

Section 13    Accidents

## Question 13.1

Mark one answer
At the scene of an accident you should

a  not put yourself at risk
b  go to those casualties who are screaming
c  pull everybody out of their vehicles
d  leave vehicle engines switched on

## Question 13.2

Mark four answers
You are the first to arrive at the scene of an accident. Which FOUR of these should you do?

a  Leave as soon as another motorist arrives
b  Switch off the vehicle engine(s)
c  Move uninjured people away from the vehicle(s)
d  Call the emergency services
e  Warn other traffic

## Question 13.3

Mark one answer
An accident has just happened. An injured person is lying in the busy road. What is the FIRST thing you should do to help?

a  Treat the person for shock
b  Warn other traffic
c  Place them in the recovery position
d  Make sure the injured person is kept warm

## Question 13.4

Mark three answers
You are the first person to arrive at an accident where people are badly injured. Which THREE should you do?

a  Switch on your own hazard warning lights
b  Make sure that someone telephones for an ambulance
c  Try and get people who are injured to drink something
d  Move the people who are injured clear of their vehicles
e  Get people who are not injured clear of the scene

## Question 13.5

Mark one answer

You arrive at the scene of a motorcycle accident. The rider is injured. When should the helmet be removed?

a  Only when it is essential
b  Always straight away
c  Only when the motorcyclist asks
d  Always, unless they are in shock

## Question 13.6

Mark three answers

You arrive at a serious motorcycle accident. The motorcyclist is unconscious and bleeding. Your main priorities should be to

a  try to stop the bleeding
b  make a list of witnesses
c  check the casualty's breathing
d  take the numbers of the vehicles involved
e  sweep up any loose debris
f  check the casualty's airways

## Question 13.7

Mark one answer

You arrive at an accident. A motorcyclist is unconscious. Your FIRST priority is the casualty's

a  breathing
b  bleeding
c  broken bones
d  bruising

## Question 13.8

Mark three answers

At an accident a casualty is unconscious. Which THREE of the following should you check urgently?

a  Circulation
b  Airway
c  Shock
d  Breathing
e  Broken bones

## Question 13.9

Mark three answers

You arrive at the scene of an accident. It has just happened and someone is unconscious. Which of the following should be given urgent priority to help them?

a   Clear the airway and keep it open
b   Try to get them to drink water
c   Check that they are breathing
d   Look for any witnesses
e   Stop any heavy bleeding
f   Take the numbers of vehicles involved

## Question 13.10

Mark three answers

At an accident someone is unconscious. Your main priorities should be to

a   sweep up the broken glass
b   take the names of witnesses
c   count the number of vehicles involved
d   check the airway is clear
e   make sure they are breathing
f   stop any heavy bleeding

## Question 13.11

Mark three answers

You have stopped at the scene of an accident to give help. Which THREE things should you do?

a   Keep injured people warm and comfortable
b   Keep injured people calm by talking to them reassuringly
c   Keep injured people on the move by walking them around
d   Give injured people a warm drink
e   Make sure that injured people are not left alone

## Question 13.12

Mark three answers

You arrive at the scene of an accident. It has just happened and someone is injured. Which THREE of the following should be given urgent priority?

a   Stop any severe bleeding
b   Get them a warm drink
c   Check that their breathing is OK
d   Take numbers of vehicles involved
e   Look for witnesses
f   Clear their airway and keep it open

## Question 13.13

Mark two answers

At an accident a casualty has stopped breathing. You should

a   remove anything that is blocking the mouth
b   keep the head tilted forwards as far as possible
c   raise the legs to help with circulation
d   try to give the casualty something to drink
e   keep the head tilted back as far as possible

## Question 13.14

Mark four answers

You are at the scene of an accident. Someone is suffering from shock. You should

a   reassure them constantly
b   offer them a cigarette
c   keep them warm
d   avoid moving them if possible
e   loosen any tight clothing
f   give them a warm drink

## Question 13.15

Mark one answer

Which of the following should you NOT do at the scene of an accident?

a   Warn other traffic by switching on your hazard warning lights
b   Call the emergency services immediately
c   Offer someone a cigarette to calm them down
d   Ask drivers to switch off their engines

## Question 13.16

Mark two answers

There has been an accident. The driver is suffering from shock. You should

a   give them a drink
b   reassure them
c   not leave them alone
d   offer them a cigarette
e   ask who caused the accident

## Question 13.17

Mark three answers
You are at the scene of an accident.
Someone is suffering from shock.
You should

a   offer them a cigarette
b   offer them a warm drink
c   keep them warm
d   loosen any tight clothing
e   reassure them constantly

## Question 13.18

Mark one answer
You have to treat someone for shock at
the scene of an accident. You should

a   reassure them constantly
b   walk them around to calm them down
c   give them something cold to drink
d   cool them down as soon as possible

## Question 13.19

Mark one answer
You arrive at the scene of a motorcycle
accident. No other vehicle is involved.
The rider is unconscious, lying in the
middle of the road. The first thing you
should do is

a   move the rider out of the road
b   warn other traffic
c   clear the road of debris
d   give the rider reassurance

## Question 13.20

Mark one answer
At an accident a small child is not
breathing. When giving mouth to mouth
you should breathe

a   sharply
b   gently
c   heavily
d   rapidly

## Question 13.21

Mark three answers
To start mouth to mouth on a casualty
you should

a   tilt their head forward
b   clear the airway
c   turn them on their side
d   tilt their head back
e   pinch the nostrils together
f   put their arms across their chest

## Question 13.22

Mark one answer
When you are giving mouth to mouth you
should only stop when

a   you think the casualty is dead
b   the casualty can breathe without help
c   the casualty has turned blue
d   you think the ambulance is coming

## Question 13.23

Mark one answer

You arrive at the scene of an accident. There has been an engine fire and someone's hands and arms have been burnt. You should NOT

a   douse the burn thoroughly with cool liquid
b   lay the casualty down
c   remove anything sticking to the burn
d   reassure them constantly

## Question 13.24

Mark one answer

You arrive at an accident where someone is suffering from severe burns. You should

a   apply lotions to the injury
b   burst any blisters
c   remove anything stuck to the burns
d   douse the burns with cool liquid

## Question 13.25

Mark two answers

You arrive at the scene of an accident. A pedestrian has a severe bleeding wound on their leg, although it is not broken. What should you do?

a   Dab the wound to stop bleeding
b   Keep both legs flat on the ground
c   Apply firm pressure to the wound
d   Raise the leg to lessen bleeding
e   Fetch them a warm drink

## Question 13.26

Mark one answer

You arrive at the scene of an accident. A passenger is bleeding badly from an arm wound. What should you do?

a   Apply pressure over the wound and keep the arm down
b   Dab the wound
c   Get them a drink
d   Apply pressure over the wound and raise the arm

## Question 13.27

<u>Mark one answer</u>
You arrive at the scene of an accident.
A pedestrian is bleeding heavily from a
leg wound but the leg is not broken.
What should you do?

a  Dab the wound to stop the bleeding
b  Keep both legs flat on the ground
c  Apply firm pressure to the wound
d  Fetch them a warm drink

## Question 13.28

<u>Mark one answer</u>
At an accident a casualty is unconscious
but still breathing. You should only move
them if

a  an ambulance is on its way
b  bystanders advise you to
c  there is further danger
d  bystanders will help you to

## Question 13.29

<u>Mark one answer</u>
At an accident you suspect a casualty
has back injuries. The area is safe. You
should

a  offer them a drink
b  not move them
c  raise their legs
d  offer them a cigarette

## Question 13.30

<u>Mark one answer</u>
At an accident it is important to look after
the casualty. When the area is safe, you
should

a  get them out of the vehicle
b  give them a drink
c  give them something to eat
d  keep them in the vehicle

## Question 13.31

<u>Mark one answer</u>
A tanker is involved in an accident.
Which sign would show that the tanker is
carrying dangerous goods?

a

b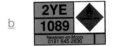

c

d

## Question 13.32

Mark three answers
The police may ask you to produce which three of these documents following an accident?

a Vehicle registration document
b Driving licence
c Theory test certificate
d Insurance certificate
e MOT test certificate
f Road tax disc

## Question 13.33

Mark one answer
At a railway level crossing the red light signal continues to flash after a train has gone by. What should you do?

a Phone the signal operator
b Alert drivers behind you
c Wait
d Proceed with caution

## Question 13.34

Mark one answer
You see a car on the hard shoulder of a motorway with a HELP pennant displayed. This means the driver is most likely to be

a a disabled person
b first aid trained
c a foreign visitor
d a rescue patrol person

## Question 13.35

Mark one answer
On the motorway, the hard shoulder should be used

a to answer a mobile phone
b when an emergency arises
c for a short rest when tired
d to check a road atlas

## Question 13.36

Mark two answers
For which TWO should you use hazard warning lights?

a When you slow down quickly on a motorway because of a hazard ahead
b When you have broken down
c When you wish to stop on double yellow lines
d When you need to park on the pavement

## Question 13.37

Mark one answer
When are you allowed to use hazard warning lights?

a  When stopped and temporarily obstructing traffic
b  When travelling during darkness without headlights
c  When parked for shopping on double yellow lines
d  When travelling slowly because you are lost

## Question 13.38

Mark one answer
You are on a motorway. A large box falls onto the road from a lorry. The lorry does not stop. You should

a  go to the next emergency telephone and inform the police
b  catch up with the lorry and try to get the driver's attention
c  stop close to the box until the police arrive
d  pull over to the hard shoulder, then remove the box

## Question 13.39

Mark one answer
There has been an accident.
A motorcyclist is lying injured and unconscious. Why should you usually not attempt to remove their helmet?

a  Because they may not want you to
b  This could result in more serious injury
c  They will get too cold if you do this
d  Because you could scratch the helmet

## Question 13.40

Mark one answer
After an accident, someone is unconscious in their vehicle. When should you call the emergency services?

a  Only as a last resort
b  As soon as possible
c  After you have woken them up
d  After checking for broken bones

## Question 13.41

Mark one answer

An accident casualty has an injured arm. They can move it freely, but it is bleeding. Why should you get them to keep it in a raised position?

a   Because it will ease the pain
b   It will help them to be seen more easily
c   To stop them touching other people
d   It will help to reduce the bleeding

## Question 13.42

Mark one answer

You are going through a congested tunnel and have to stop. What should you do?

a   Pull up very close to the vehicle in front to save space
b   Ignore any message signs as they are never up to date
c   Keep a safe distance from the vehicle in front
d   Make a U-turn and find another route

## Question 13.43

Mark one answer

You are going through a tunnel. What should you look out for that warns of accidents or congestion?

a   Hazard warning lines
b   Other drivers flashing their lights
c   Variable message signs
d   Areas marked with hatch markings

## Question 13.44

Mark one answer

You are going through a tunnel. What systems are provided to warn of any accidents or congestion?

a   Double white centre lines
b   Variable message signs
c   Chevron 'distance markers'
d   Rumble strips

## Question 13.45

Mark one answer
While driving, a warning light on your
vehicle's instrument panel comes on.
You should

a continue if the engine sounds alright
b hope that it is just a temporary
  electrical fault
c deal with the problem when there is
  more time
d check out the problem quickly and
  safely

## Question 13.46

Mark one answer
You have broken down on a two-way
road. You have a warning triangle. You
should place the warning triangle at least
how far from your vehicle?

a 5 metres (16 feet)
b 25 metres (82 feet)
c 45 metres (147 feet)
d 100 metres (328 feet)

## Question 13.47

Mark three answers
You break down on a level crossing. The
lights have not yet begun to flash. Which
THREE things should you do?

a Telephone the signal operator
b Leave your vehicle and get everyone
  clear
c Walk down the track and signal the
  next train
d Move the vehicle if a signal operator
  tells you to
e Tell drivers behind what has
  happened

## Question 13.48

Mark one answer
Your vehicle has broken down on an
automatic railway level crossing. What
should you do FIRST?

a Get everyone out of the vehicle and
  clear of the crossing
b Phone the signal operator so that
  trains can be stopped
c Walk along the track to give warning
  to any approaching trains
d Try to push the vehicle clear of the
  crossing as soon as possible

## Question 13.49

Mark two answers

Your tyre bursts while you are driving. Which TWO things should you do?

a  Pull on the handbrake
b  Brake as quickly as possible
c  Pull up slowly at the side of the road
d  Hold the steering wheel firmly to keep control
e  Continue on at a normal speed

## Question 13.50

Mark two answers

Which TWO things should you do when a front tyre bursts?

a  Apply the handbrake to stop the vehicle
b  Brake firmly and quickly
c  Let the vehicle roll to a stop
d  Hold the steering wheel lightly
e  Grip the steering wheel firmly

## Question 13.51

Mark one answer

Your vehicle has a puncture on a motorway. What should you do?

a  Drive slowly to the next service area to get assistance
b  Pull up on the hard shoulder. Change the wheel as quickly as possible
c  Pull up on the hard shoulder. Use the emergency phone to get assistance
d  Switch on your hazard lights. Stop in your lane

## Question 13.52

Mark three answers

Which of these items should you carry in your vehicle for use in the event of an accident?

a  Road map
b  Can of petrol
c  Jump leads
d  Fire extinguisher
e  First Aid kit
f  Warning triangle

237

## Question 13.53

Mark one answer

You are in an accident on a two-way road. You have a warning triangle with you. At what distance before the obstruction should you place the warning triangle?

a   25 metres (82 feet)
b   45 metres (147 feet)
c   100 metres (328 feet)
d   150 metres (492 feet)

## Question 13.54

Mark one answer

You have broken down on a two-way road. You have a warning triangle. It should be displayed

a   on the roof of your vehicle
b   at least 150 metres (492 feet) behind your vehicle
c   at least 45 metres (147 feet) behind your vehicle
d   just behind your vehicle

## Question 13.55

Mark one answer

You have stalled in the middle of a level crossing and cannot restart the engine. The warning bell starts to ring. You should

a   get out and clear of the crossing
b   run down the track to warn the signal operator
c   carry on trying to restart the engine
d   push the vehicle clear of the crossing

## Question 13.56

Mark one answer

You are on the motorway. Luggage falls from your vehicle. What should you do?

a   Stop at the next emergency telephone and contact the police
b   Stop on the motorway and put on hazard lights while you pick it up
c   Walk back up the motorway to pick it up
d   Pull up on the hard shoulder and wave traffic down

## Question 13.57

Mark two answers

You are on a motorway. When can you use hazard warning lights?

a When a vehicle is following too closely
b When you slow down quickly because of danger ahead
c When you are towing another vehicle
d When driving on the hard shoulder
e When you have broken down on the hard shoulder

## Question 13.58

Mark four answers

You are involved in an accident with another vehicle. Someone is injured. Your vehicle is damaged. Which FOUR of the following should you find out?

a Whether the driver owns the other vehicle involved
b The other driver's name, address and telephone number
c The make and registration number of the other vehicle
d The occupation of the other driver
e The details of the other driver's vehicle insurance
f Whether the other driver is licensed to drive

## Question 13.59

Mark three answers

You have broken down on a motorway. When you use the emergency telephone you will be asked

a for the number on the telephone that you are using
b for your driving licence details
c for the name of your vehicle insurance company
d for details of yourself and your vehicle
e whether you belong to a motoring organisation

## Question 13.60

Mark one answer

You lose control of your car and damage a garden wall. No one is around. What must you do?

a Report the accident to the police within 24 hours
b Go back to tell the house owner the next day
c Report the accident to your insurance company when you get home
d Find someone in the area to tell them about it immediately

## Question 13.61

Mark one answer
Your engine catches fire. What should you do first?

a  Lift the bonnet and disconnect the battery
b  Lift the bonnet and warn other traffic
c  Call the breakdown service
d  Call the fire brigade

## Question 13.62

Mark one answer
Before driving through a tunnel what should you do?

a  Switch your radio off
b  Remove any sunglasses
c  Close your sunroof
d  Switch on windscreen wipers

## Question 13.63

Mark one answer
You are driving through a tunnel and the traffic is flowing normally. What should you do?

a  Use parking lights
b  Use front spot lights
c  Use dipped headlights
d  Use rear fog lights

## Question 13.64

Mark one answer
Before entering a tunnel it is good advice to

a  put on your sunglasses
b  check tyre pressures
c  change to a lower gear
d  tune your radio to a local channel

## Question 13.65

Mark one answer
You are driving through a tunnel. Your vehicle breaks down. What should you do?

a  Switch on hazard warning lights
b  Remain in your vehicle
c  Wait for the police to find you
d  Rely on CCTV cameras seeing you

## Question 13.66

Mark one answer
Your vehicle breaks down in a tunnel. What should you do?

a  Stay in your vehicle and wait for the police
b  Stand in the lane behind your vehicle to warn others
c  Stand in front of your vehicle to warn oncoming drivers
d  Switch on hazard lights then go and call for help immediately

## Question 13.67

Mark one answer
You have an accident while driving through a tunnel. You are not injured but your vehicle cannot be driven. What should you do first?

a   Rely on other drivers phoning for the police
b   Switch off the engine and switch on hazard lights
c   Take the names of witnesses and other drivers
d   Sweep up any debris that is in the road

## Question 13.68

Mark one answer
When driving through a tunnel you should

a   Look out for variable message signs
b   Use your air conditioning system
c   Switch on your rear fog lights
d   Always use your windscreen wipers

## Question 13.69

Mark two answers
What TWO safeguards could you take against fire risk to your vehicle?

a   Keep water levels above maximum
b   Carry a fire extinguisher
c   Avoid driving with a full tank of petrol
d   Use unleaded petrol
e   Check out any strong smell of petrol
f   Use low octane fuel

## Answers and explanations

13.1   a

13.2   b, c, d, e

13.3   b Warning other traffic first helps stop the accident getting even worse.

13.4   a, b, e

13.5   a

13.6   a, c, f
Injuries should be dealt with in the order Airway, Breathing then Circulation and bleeding.

13.7   a

13.8   a, b, d

13.9   a, c, e
Note that these are the things to which you should give urgent priority.

13.10  d, e, f

13.11  a, b, e
You should not move injured people unless they are in danger; nor should you give them anything to drink.

13.12  a, c, f

13.13  a, e

13.14  a, c, d, e

13.15  c

13.16  b, c

13.17  c, d, e

13.18  a

13.19  b Note that this is the FIRST thing to do. By warning other traffic you help reduce the risk of more collisions.

13.20  b

13.21  b, d, e

13.22  b

13.23  c

13.24  d

13.25  c, d

13.26  d

13.27  c

13.28  c

13.29  b If you move the casualty you may worsen their injury.

13.30  d

13.31  b

13.32  b, d, e

13.33  c This usually means another train is coming.

13.34  a

13.35  b

13.36  a, b

13.37  a

13.38  a

13.39  b

13.40  b

13.41  d

13.42  c

13.43  c

13.44  b

13.45  d

13.46  c 45 metres is recommended on two-way roads and 150 metres on a dual carriageway. You should not use a warning triangle on a motorway; it is too dangerous.

13.47  a, b, d

13.48  a Your first action is to get everyone to safety.

13.49  c, d
You will need both hands firmly on the wheel in order to control the car, and using the gears or brakes is likely to make your

car swerve. When possible, it is
safest just to let your car roll to
a halt at the side of the road.

13.50 c, e

13.51 c The hard shoulder of a
motorway is a dangerous place
and 'c' is the safest course of
action. It can be particularly
dangerous to try to change an
offside wheel as you may be
very close to fast-moving traffic
in the left-hand lane.

13.52 d, e, f

13.53 b

13.54 c

13.55 a A train may arrive within
seconds so 'a' is the only safe
possibility.

13.56 a

13.57 b, e

13.58 a, b, c, e

13.59 a, d, e

13.60 a

13.61 d

13.62 b

13.63 c

13.64 d Local radio will inform you of
any breakdowns and congestion
in the tunnel.

13.65 a

13.66 d

13.67 b

13.68 a

13.69 b, e

# Theory Test Questions
# for Car Drivers

## 2004–2005

Section 14    Vehicle loading

## Question 14.1

Mark two answers

You are towing a small trailer on a busy three-lane motorway. All the lanes are open. You must

a   not exceed 60mph
b   not overtake
c   have a stabiliser fitted
d   use only the left and centre lanes

## Question 14.2

Mark one answer

Any load that is carried on a roof rack MUST be

a   securely fastened when driving
b   carried only when strictly necessary
c   as light as possible
d   covered with plastic sheeting

## Question 14.3

Mark one answer

You are planning to tow a caravan. Which of these will mostly help to aid the vehicle handling?

a   A jockey-wheel fitted to the towbar
b   Power steering fitted to the towing vehicle
c   Anti-lock brakes fitted to the towing vehicle
d   A stabiliser fitted to the towbar

## Question 14.4

Mark one answer

If a trailer swerves or snakes when you are towing it you should

a   ease off the accelerator and reduce your speed
b   let go of the steering wheel and let it correct itself
c   brake hard and hold the pedal down
d   increase your speed as quickly as possible

## Question 14.5

Mark one answer

How can you stop a caravan snaking from side to side?

a   Turn the steering wheel slowly to each side
b   Accelerate to increase your speed
c   Stop as quickly as you can
d   Slow down very gradually

## Question 14.6

Mark two answers
On which TWO occasions might you inflate your tyres to more than the recommended normal pressure?

a   When the roads are slippery
b   When driving fast for a long distance
c   When the tyre tread is worn below 2mm
d   When carrying a heavy load
e   When the weather is cold
f   When the vehicle is fitted with anti-lock brakes

## Question 14.7

Mark one answer
A heavy load on your roof rack will

a   improve the road holding
b   reduce the stopping distance
c   make the steering lighter
d   reduce stability

## Question 14.8

Mark one answer
Are passengers allowed to ride in a caravan that is being towed?

a   Yes if they are over fourteen
b   No not at any time
c   Only if all the seats in the towing vehicle are full
d   Only if a stabilizer is fitted

## Question 14.9

Mark one answer
You are towing a caravan along a motorway. The caravan begins to swerve from side to side. What should you do?

a   Ease off the accelerator slowly
b   Steer sharply from side to side
c   Do an emergency stop
d   Speed up very quickly

## Question 14.10

Mark one answer
A trailer must stay securely hitched-up to the towing vehicle. What additional safety device can be fitted to the trailer braking system?

a   Stabiliser
b   Jockey wheel
c   Corner steadies
d   Breakaway cable

247

## Question 14.11

Mark two answers
Overloading your vehicle can seriously affect the

a   gearbox
b   steering
c   handling
d   battery life
e   journey time

## Question 14.12

Mark one answer
Who is responsible for making sure that a vehicle is not overloaded?

a   The driver of the vehicle
b   The owner of the items being carried
c   The person who loaded the vehicle
d   The licensing authority

## Question 14.13

Mark one answer
Which of these is a suitable restraint for a child under three years?

a   A child seat
b   An adult holding a child
c   An adult seat belt
d   A lap belt

## Question 14.14

Mark one answer
A child under three years is being carried in your vehicle. They should be secured in a restraint. Which of these is suitable?

a   An adult holding a child
b   A lap belt
c   A baby carrier
d   An adult seat belt

## Answers and explanations

14.1   a, d
14.2   a The word 'MUST' in the question makes 'a' correct.
14.3   d
14.4   a Options 'b', 'c' or 'd' would all be likely to make the problem worse
14.5   d
14.6   b, d
14.7   d A heavy load on the roof will shift the centre of gravity of your vehicle and could make you more likely to skid or roll over.
14.8   b
14.9   a
14.10  d
14.11  b, c
14.12  a
14.13  a
14.14  c